MIRANDA INNES'

COUNTRY HOME

BOOK

MIRANDA INNES'

COUNTRY HOME

BOOK

A practical guide to restoring and decorating in the country style

PHOTOGRAPHY BY SPIKE POWELL

SIMON AND SCHUSTER
New York · London · Toronto · Sydney · Tokyo

A Dorling Kindersley Book

Senior Art Editor: Nick Harris
Project Editor: Josephine Buchanan
Technical Advisor and Designer: Mustafa Sami
Managing Editor: David Lamb
Art Director: Roger Bristow

Simon and Schuster
Simon & Schuster Building
Rockefeller Center
1230 Avenue of the Americas
New York, New York 10020

First published in 1989 in Great Britain by
Dorling Kindersley Limited,
9 Henrietta Street, London WC2E 8PS

Printed and bound in West Germany by Mohndruck GmbH,
Gütersloh
1   3   5   7   9   10   8   6   4   2

Contents

A Sense of the Country

"A PLACE IN THE COUNTRY", like "a summer afternoon", is the sort of phrase that evokes a misty-eyed and dreamy response. "The country" is symbolic of a different way of life from that which most people endure. In a sense, the city embodies an embarrassment of riches: it requires discipline to enjoy what you have because there is always a quiet but insistent pressure to go out and get more, or do more. There is a competitive spirit in the town or city; all the myriad things you could be doing somehow mitigate the pleasure of what you are doing.

But the country is altogether different. Life doesn't race past in the same way – things happen at a slower pace. There is time to savor the moment, to plan ahead and enjoy the expectation of events, and to relive them in hindsight. You are not faced with endless multiple-choice decisions, which are eventually as laborious as they are initially exhilarating.

The country throws you on your own resources and encourages the nurture and care of objects, relationships and events – there may be less to choose from, but what and who there is become proportionately more significant.

The nineteenth-century English cleric Sydney Smith, who was consigned to the country for, as he felt, far too long, said in a letter to a friend: "I have no relish for the country; it is a kind of healthy grave", and was concerned that it was a place "where creation will expire before tea-time".

Do-it-yourself (LEFT) *Thoughtful craftsmanship plays a large role in country decoration. These ingenious shutters have been made with a piece of hand-painted stained glass.*

But William Cowper, the eighteenth-century writer, best expresses the feelings of the confirmed country-lover, when he wrote: "God made the country and man made the town". And so it is. If you happen to have the good fortune to be able to throw open your door and step into a field bordered by scarlet autumn maples, or fling open a window and hear nothing beyond bees, birds and a distant tractor, you will have found the perfect standard by which to measure daily tribulations. There is nothing like an uninterrupted view of lake or mountain or green fields to put the gas bill into its proper perspective.

❦ Living in the Country ❧

Living in the country implies a relaxation of the barriers between indoors and out. Although only a romantic fool would advertise casual accessibility to passing burglars, a house in the country does not need quite the defensive vigilance of a city dwelling. Doors and windows can be left open so that the smell of roses can waft into the kitchen, and dogs and cats can waft out.

A house in the country can have a liberating feeling of unconfined space. It is possible to have a bedroom on the ground floor, with huge windows to leave open on summer nights; or a conservatory in which you can sit even in mid-winter and admire a view of trees, or topiary or frozen lake. Beyond the house itself are other ways to make the most of space – the conversion of a barn into a galleried great hall; or the introduction of a Chekovian summerhouse by the apple trees, where you can sit and meditate.

In the country you can enjoy the pleasures of peace and quiet: of sitting out under the stars on a clear summer night; or taking your breakfast out through the kitchen door to a sunny patch of grass under the cherry tree; or the breath-stopping beauty of waking up to the perfect whiteness of snow, unbesludged by traffic.

Cloistered calm (LEFT) *A collection of elderly wicker chairs creates a typically laid-back country scene. These chairs were bought over the years at junk shops and have been renovated by spray paint in sympathetic toning colors.*

Country crafts (LEFT INSET) *Handcrafted objects cast a particular magic: these doves were carved as a wedding present for the couple who live here. The window frame was painted olive green and has faded to a warm gray that complements the walls beautifully.*

But if you do live in the country, you are one of the lucky ones – many people find themselves marooned in city or town. They are tethered to work, with a tiny garden, a view of their neighbor from the windows, and the blackbird's song drowned by the thunder of buses.

Fortunately, there is a look – almost an attitude – that evokes the country at its best. It has to do with celebrating what you have, looking at your home and your possessions with a fresh eye and exploiting their particular charms. It is a tradition that is strong on ingenuity – if time is short, there are shortcuts and theatrical flourishes that can be effective, bringing an air of country pleasure to the most unpromising town flat. Even if your home is in a town, you can give its decoration and furnishings a country look.

❧ THE COUNTRY LOOK ☙

A COUNTRY LOOK IS ONE composed of natural materials and country colors. It is an eclectic and organic look that grows and changes – as you pick up a Yorkshire kitchen dresser at an auction, an antique at a sale, or some rich paisley-patterned wallpaper in a little shop on your travels. At one extreme, it is a look that can absorb the clutter of

Windows on the world
(LEFT) *Little windows pierce the massive walls of this converted Martello Tower in the East of England. Each window frames the seascape* *beyond: a perfect antidote to city chaos. Here, the run of steps exaggerates the perspective and provides a convenient display area for a few simple objects.*

Splendor in the suburbs
(ABOVE) *Less than an hour outside New York city, this early twentieth-century house has a definite rustic air. It is surrounded by trees* *and enough space in which to enjoy an outdoor life. Pastel 1920s junk-shop furniture and fabric are refreshing and reflect the general mood of the house.*

presents given to you by affectionate friends over the last few decades; a look that takes its cue from a spectrum of the good things in life, spanning a kaleidoscope of pattern, color, scent and texture. At the other extreme, it can embrace the puritan and pared-down simplicity of the contemplative's cell: stone floor, solid furniture and humble fabrics. Each aspect expresses character and a part of the natural world outside.

ᙦ A Sense of History ᙨ

A COUNTRY LOOK IMPLIES a sense of care and history. Furniture is not necessarily new, but it is cleaned and polished and loved – a vast, scrubbed kitchen table, the scene of many winter evening feasts of scones and crumpets, or an old sagging Chesterfield that has borne three generations of wriggling children and been re-covered countless times. These are the pieces that have earned a permanent place in family mythology and affections and sit comfortably in your home.

The country look has to do with authenticity, with a preference for the quirky and un-labor-saving genuine article, although this should be pursued within reason: only a fanatical purist

Simple window dressing
(LEFT) *This house is on the edge of a sizable town, but a relaxed outdoor feeling is achieved by exploiting views of the garden. The windows are unadorned except for a miniature echo of the street outside, arranged on the molding.*

Country comes to town
(ABOVE) *This house sits in the heart of London, but it has a decidedly rural air – created by an autumnal palette of polished wood and russet carpet, masses of dried flowers and the elderly Bargello tapestry that covers the chair.*

would eschew a discreet and blessedly functional dishwasher in favor of a kitchen sink and washing suds. A sense of relaxed calm is the look to aim for, so whatever makes the day-to-day business of life less onerous should be welcomed.

Above all, a country look is user-friendly. It has to do with open door and windows, bringing the outdoors in with great bunches of lilac or spring blossoms or scarlet and green Christmas wreaths. Mud and rain and dust, armfuls of roses, baskets of earthy vegetables, dogs, children and visitors, all bring something of the outside in. So the general sense is of welcome, warmth and tolerance.

❧ PERIOD AUTHENTICITY ☙

THERE ARE SOME FACTS about your home that cannot be changed. Few people (outside America) are bold enough to change the location of their home – to transport the skeleton of their barn from Berkshire in England to Brownsville in Texas. The other immutable fact is the period in which your home was built. Ancient buildings need to be converted with care and sympathy. The older the building, the more likely it is to have tiny windows and low ceilings, either of which you change at your peril. It is an unkind and thankless task to wrench an Elizabethan timber-frame cottage into the twentieth century by changing its doors, floors and windows, thereby destroying its original character.

The most important point to bear in mind when you make any plans for restoring or decorating your home is that only the appropriate prospers. Often the most comfortable choice of furnishing and decoration is that which evolved with the house – hand-painted Chinoiserie wallpaper will look divine in your small Regency palace, but sadly at odds with a tiny-windowed stone-walled croft. Dark, carved furniture and roughly plastered walls are perfect for a modest Jacobean dwelling, but definitely uncomfortable in a streamlined piece of 1930s architecture.

❧ ENJOYING THE AGE OF YOUR HOME ☙

PLAY UP THE AGE and character of your home. Enjoy its Edwardian solidity, its colonial grace, or its frontier strength. If yours is an ancient cottage, visit the local churches of the same vintage, in which you may find an inspirational sourcebook of decorative color and design, possibly applied by the same hands as put your house together.

A room with a view
(LEFT) *If you have a spectacular view, exploit it. The owners of this ground-floor bedroom have installed French windows that can be thrown open to frame a glorious expanse of countryside. Together with the classically-inspired semicircular window, they fill the room with light and air. A screen stops mosquitoes and other undesirables from entering at night.*

Making an exit (ABOVE)
Country homes have a liberating feeling of spaciousness because of their easy access to the outside world. This door invites you to step into a meadow with a froth of golden flowers. The owners of this home have also made the roof into an outdoor sitting space, where they can revel in spectacular views from the comfort of a glazed sun room.

If possible, for any scheme to restore your home to its particular period, similar materials to the original fabric of the building should be used. Neighborhood snooping is helpful before you begin any restoration task – to see how local floors were laid, or how particular screen walls were finished. Occasionally, it may lead to the discovery of an Aladdin's cave of nicely worn authentic materials from a building due for demolition. Make a friend of the local builder, visit the nearest auction house, and keep a curious eye open for handwritten "for sale" notices when you drive along the lanes and byways in the country.

There is no specific period that encapsulates the country look. Brand new buildings, particularly if

Sympathetic decoration
(LEFT) *This turn-of-the-century house on the Hudson river has been simply painted in warm colors to complement its clean proportions and to contrast with the cool expanse of water outside.*

Rejuvenating an old farm
(ABOVE) *Old materials work hard in this farmhouse: tiles for the floor were collected locally, the kitchen units were put together from old wood, and a marble-topped washstand serves as a pastry slab.*

Character-forming (LEFT) *Whatever the period of your home, find and exploit its essential character. This late eighteenth-century Martello Tower, one of many built around the coast of Britain to repel Napoleon, has thick fortress walls and a solid masculinity. Painting the giant brick arches plain white is all that is required to emphasize the strength of the place.*

Traditional walls (LEFT INSET) *A tweedy combination of English brick and flints is typical of old Norfolk houses. The door – which is not used – came from a local architectural salvage yard.*

Faking age (RIGHT) *The couple who built this house a year before this picture was taken wanted something akin to an old French farmhouse, so they used original materials wherever possible. Old bricks were used for the hearth and old beams were rescued from a derelict building.*

they are built with simplicity and a sense of tradition, can embody the look just as well as little thatched masterpieces from the sixteenth century. The key to countrification is a choice of sympathetic materials – rough plaster, old beams, wood-framed windows, and slate floors. The vernacular country (even peasant) architecture of Italy, France and Greece could not be more simply constructed, but frequently it achieves perfect grace, proportion and livability with nothing more than a humble pile of breeze blocks.

Similarly, clapboard houses often embody natural elegance that spans the centuries. Even contemporary versions look good – there is a repertoire of traditional features in America that gives a modern version a convincing quality of years of history.

Of course, it is possible to fake a particular period, but successful faking needs to be approached with the seriousness that any other kind of forgery requires – a lot of homework in archives and libraries. Additions to old buildings must be carefully considered and carried out with respect. The general proportions of floor to window to ceiling should be echoed; it is all too easy to become obsessed with the prospect of extra space and cling to the idea you first thought of, without exploring other – less disruptive – possibilities.

❧ APPROPRIATE FIXTURES ❧

EVEN IN THE BEST regulated houses, from time to time things will need changing or modernizing. You may suddenly find yourself in the middle of a family uprising – a violent rebellion against

living in chill authentically, warmed only by an attractive but moody stove. Before you reach, with frozen hand, for the local paper and the name of the nearest plumber, you would do well to consider alternatives to standard modern heating systems for your home.

❧ THE BEST OF THE PAST ❧

THERE WAS A TIME, at the end of the nineteenth century, when radiators were considered a cause for celebration and were created as works of art – large and serviceable with a flurry of embossed art nouveau leaves. Again, in the 1920s and 1930s, radiators were made to stand large and proud and unashamed. Subsequently, heating engineers have become diffident about their creations. Now we have radiators that may take up the same, if not a larger amount of wall space, but they look like chunks of industrial jetsam.

There are two solutions. The preferable one is to find good, old-fashioned solid radiators; the second is to camouflage contemporary radiators, by using cunning paint color, or by boxing them in with a lid on the top (see page 166).

Finding the right radiator (LEFT) *Originally, radiators were not hidden away in embarrassment: they were solid articles of furniture, made to be seen. This chunky cast-iron radiator functions perfectly and contributes a certain period charm to its turn of the century home. The child's chair – made from hickory sticks – is also early twentieth-century.*

Restoring an original hearth (ABOVE) *A genuine inglenook, with an integral seat and shelf for a salt container, has been blackened by years of smoke. It now houses a responsive and effective wood-burning stove – appropriate heating for life in a wooded corner of the English countryside.*

Fortress door (ABOVE) *This hefty door, complete with its original massive hinges and bar, fits perfectly in a converted Martello Tower on the coast of England: its solid proportions were designed to resist the battering of invading armies.*

New home for an old door (LEFT) *This magnificent door is of dubious origin but now its ancient charm makes it a welcome ingredient in the lobby of a country house. Its subtle markings are shown to good effect against bare plank walls.*

Country cooking (RIGHT) *The warm heart of a home is the classic solid-fuel cooker. This is a particularly handsome model, part of an attractive and functional kitchen that is full of good ideas. Note the heavy, unglazed floor tiles that are also used (sealed) as a worktop surface.*

In fact, handsome modern radiators do exist. There are classy and inventive models for heating and drying towels in the bathroom, which do double duty in the kitchen drying tea-cloths. Though ideally you have a geriatric rise-and-fall airer over your stove, permanently festooned with a tasteful display of striped cloths.

Which brings us to the solid fuel stove, the essential element of country cuisine. It gives a wonderful feeling of warmth and security and has a comforting, matronly presence. It is unbeaten for good looks, even if speed is not its forte. Because it requires a definite and particular approach to cooking the best thing to do is to look around first, to discover whether it is going to suit your lifestyle.

Doors are another element that can have a strong effect on the character of your home. If you have to change or replace a door you will discover that there is no shortage of charming old doors to be found, but you may well be driven mad in the

Framing a window (LEFT)
One way of evoking the country spirit is to play up attractive architectural features. In this early twentieth-century home the owner has outlined the rounded window with a filet of delicate stenciling. The strange nest-like object on the neighboring mantelpiece is in fact a "mixed media" basket, concocted from an extraordinary ragbag of paper strips, old film and plastic – a gentle dig at a consumer society.

Dramatic paint effects
(RIGHT) *This house is expressive of its compulsive decorator-owner – walls, ceiling, windows, picture frames and floor have all been embellished with some kind of paint virtuosity. A tiny room like this is a good opportunity to experiment with dramatic finishes – these walls are combed in two directions on top of a contrasting color (see page 80 for combing).*

search for the appropriate door to fit the doorway that you have in mind. Not only do the vertical and horizontal measurements have to tally, but the new door should also open the same way and be of the same thickness as the old, otherwise the hinges will be bothersome. Don't give up and settle for the hideous, coarse, panelled door that you saw in the local DIY shop – a good door can add more character than you would imagine.

One answer to the problem is to change the dimensions of the doorway to fit the perfect door. Alternatively, in nineteenth-century houses you can often exchange existing doors, replacing the more prominent ones that have been vandalized with similar, unmutilated ones from less obvious places elsewhere in the house.

✺ PAINT EFFECTS ✺

UNTIL THE INVENTION of easily available wallpaper in the last century, paint was all there was with which to decorate walls. Partly as a result of this, any other form of decoration looks out of place in houses of a certain age – not necessarily unsuccessful, just inauthentic.

Paint effects still have the charm that has always characterized them. Once you have escaped from the dogma of matte magnolia, you will never want to return. Ragging and dragging, dry-brushing and sponging are all so easy, and the repertoire of different paints and glazes allows you to achieve such subtlety and depth of color, such shading and intensity and transparency, that you will find flat color very resistible.

Part of the appeal, as well as the horror of painting lies in the fact that you cannot possibly predict what the final effect will be. The room will change dramatically as you paint the last coat and it all ties together; sunshine will affect the color quite differently from artificial light; painting the ceiling and finishing the floor will alter the impact of the walls, and so too will furniture and paintings. If you are by nature extremely cautious, you might feel happier experimenting on a sheet of hardboard before you commit yourself to tackling wall or ceiling. Or, like a dancer limbering up, it is a good idea to loosen up by beginning with what is euphemistically known as the smallest room. It will not really matter too much what it looks like, since no one spends a huge amount of time there and it is not a major problem to overpaint a disaster. And the smaller the room the quicker you can finish it and witness the magic of completion. While you are still buoyed by euphoria, you can race off to transform the kitchen or bedroom.

❦ DECORATING WITH FABRICS ❧

FURTHER TRANSFORMATIONS can be achieved quickly and easily with fabrics – another area where a touch of theater is effective. Fabrics are useful to soften, blur and blend; to give a feeling of warmth and welcome; and to link color and pattern in a room.

To perform this magic, fabrics do not have to be new or expensive, although it has to be said that a poor quality fabric – particularly that with a high synthetic content – has an irritating way of advertising itself. For the country look, it is best always to go for an easy generosity of a natural material that

DECORATIVE
BORDER (*page 87*)

PAINTED TABLE TOP
(*page 140*)

USING A BLOCK
(*page 94*)

STENCILED
FLOORBOARDS
(*page 50*)

Colorwashing (LEFT) *Colorwashing is a simple technique (see page 78) that can provide the perfect foil to more detailed decoration – this wash of burnt umber over white is disciplined by a whimsical potato print border of blue oil paint.*

The pleasure of painting (ABOVE) *Painting is the most ancient and satisfying art; once you discover its joys, your house and its contents will become a clamor of bare canvases, demanding color. Here are some of the techniques shown in this book.*

will drape and age well: cottons and linens, wool and even hessian are the perfect country materials. They come in a variety of weights and textures: from the soft billows of muslin to crisp chintz formality, from the unwieldy stiffness of heavy upholstery linen to the flowing transparency of fine handkerchief linen.

❦ USING FABRICS ❦

ONCE YOU HAVE CHOSEN a fabric, the next stage is to exploit its particular qualities. Soft, lightweight fabrics respond well to gathers and drape beautifully in a way reminiscent of the fluted robes of classical sculpture. Heavy, stiff furnishing fabrics need to be bullied to achieve an interesting line – curtains need to hang down on to the ground so that their folds are broken.

Upholstery looks best when it has a framework of piping. Carefully-made loose covers have an unpretentious country air and a comfortable feeling of permanence. Such covers need time and skill to achieve, but luckily there are alternatives you might consider that do not rely on bindings and neatly-sewn seams. If you have soft blankets in strong colors, or lengths of paisley, or a handsome old quilt or two, you can throw them casually across an armchair and confect a cover in minutes.

Such ingenuity is a traditional trait of the country dweller. Fabrics in the past did not make single appearances but came back again and again in various guises – as quilts, rugs or patchwork. These old arts of needlework may seem anachronistic in the modern age of instant gratification, but they have much to recommend them. Making a patchwork quilt, for example, takes some beating for its calming and therapeutic value. And the results of your labors are unmatched for their comforting evocation of tranquillity and leisure.

FURNISHING COTTON

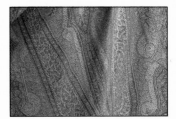

ANTIQUE PAISLEY

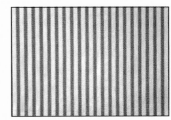

COTTON TICKING

Mixing prints (LEFT) *A bedroom can look fresh and pretty with a harmonious confetti of tiny flower prints – the curtain fabric here is echoed by country print wallpaper and bedlinen. Generous amounts of white in the room keep the effect clean rather than cloying.*

Bedroom fabrics (ABOVE) *These fabrics are drawn from a variety of traditional sources: hand-woven Quaker lace at the window, soft English lace pillows, a cotton wedding bedcover, and a faded Swedish appliqué quilt. A painted brass and iron bed completes a perfect guest room.*

Freshness by the meter (ABOVE) *Clever use of color in fabrics transforms the atmosphere of a room. A combination of blue and white cannot help but recreate a feeling of airy high summer, just as the kaleidoscopic richness of paisley has a sense of warmth that suits winter firelight.*

Small-scale decorating
(ABOVE) *Stenciled decoration is typical of American folk art and transforms old furniture – like this battered tin logbox.*

Simple furniture (LEFT)
Functional furniture is given dramatic definition by a rich crimson background. This table is a Pennsylvanian butcher's block, above which hangs an old Spanish plate rack.

Bedroom furniture (RIGHT)
Country fabrics can mollify the harshness of solid wood furniture. This carved German four-poster bed is softened by delicate linen and lace pillows and a muted patchwork quilt.

The stage is set: you have restored your home in keeping with its period, replaced modern fitments, and added a dash of theater with paint and fabric.

❧ COUNTRY FURNITURE ❧

NOW YOUR FURNITURE takes over the domestic narrative; expansive, comfortable furniture, chosen with a fastidious eye and lovingly cared for to give a sense of welcome and well-being.

Furniture that works best in a country setting is solid and simple. Anathema to a calm and countrified air of relaxation are little pieces of fussy furniture wobbling on unsteady legs, just waiting for the tail-wag of a passing dog to topple them over; or too much furniture, through which you thread your way with difficulty; or shiny and vulnerable veneer; or fidgety reproduction chairs and tables with spindly carved cabriole legs stained an unconvincing walnut color; or little bits and pieces of occasional furniture that clog and fester around a room, taking up living space.

Better to simplify, taking inspiration from the Shaker communities in nineteenth-century America who hung everything possible on the walls – shelves, cupboards, even folding chairs and tables were hung somewhere inconspicuous to leave as much free floor-space as possible.

Country furniture is almost by definition solid and functional, but an element of joyousness has traditionally come from added color – from flowered chintz upholstery, to painted wooden cupboards and stenciled chairs. One of the virtues of a

Flaunting it (LEFT) *Every spare surface can take displays – even the sideboard here is composed of richly-colored Victorian tiles. Mirrors and glass prevent the room feeling too claustrophobic.*

Collecting folk art (ABOVE) *This pair of whimsical Holsteins were hand-carved in Pennsylvania and are a charming example of the folk art that is alive and well in America.*

classic country look is that it can tolerate rebellion. So you can jazz up the general air of worthiness of very plain furniture with one or two touches of 1930s color, or crisp lacquered chinoiserie.

❧ COLLECTABLES ❧

WHAT PEOPLE COLLECT, and the way that they display their treasures, are fascinating insights into character. These collections are the agreeable obsessions that rouse you early on Sunday mornings to hunt through antique markets and have you nervously bidding for job lots at a local auction.

The character of a collection is built up almost imperceptibly – you may not even notice that a collection is forming at all. But having realized that you have surreptitiously amassed a small flock of china swans or classic Staffordshire jugs, the least you can do is to display them to their best advantage, and expect to be given a whole lot more as Christmases and birthdays come round.

The secret of effective display is to differentiate between storage and display. If everything is permanently on show, then the result may be claustrophobic. But if you can put all the multi-colored jugs away and just keep out the blue and white ones, then there is a chance of glorious harmony.

Busy areas should be carefully contained. A pinboard encrusted with precious trivia will have meaning and drama only if it is given a space to itself, not if it has to do battle with a Welsh dresser close by, which is in its turn groaning with a rainbow-colored load of plates and cups. Each area should be framed by a restful area of plain wall.

Rural sophistication (LEFT)
The country look thrives on the meeting of opposites: this is an irreverent marriage of sacred and profane. A small cherubic Atlas bears a marble slab, upon which stands an ecclesiastical lamp – quite at home amidst backdoor clutter. The grand-looking marble jigsaw floor is actually extremely practical and cost next to nothing; it was made from monumental masonry offcuts, embedded in concrete.

Rustic simplicity (RIGHT)
Here everything is simple and natural – from the herringbone brick floor and soft gray clapboard walls, to the humble ticking on the sofa and the white painted wicker chair. This is an unpretentious formula that exudes a restful air of calm relaxation. It is a look that relies on careful forethought – the warm and welcoming glow is due to the fact that the room was planned to take full advantage of the path of the setting sun.

Think precise – wooden kitchen implements in a terracotta pot with the odd bit of quarry tile and wood can be attractive in their own right, but the intrusion of a single yellowed plastic spatula in the composition will reduce a promising still life to an untidy bunch of kitchen equipment.

ᴓ THE COUNTRY SPIRIT ᴓᴄ

A LOOK OF THE COUNTRY is one that makes you feel good; that promises welcome and absolves you from unnecessary worries. Everyone, even the most confirmed urban sophisticate, has a bit of the country within – a longing for fresh air and open spaces, and for the time to appreciate the pleasures of home as a loving and peaceful refuge. We all need reminders of the passing seasons and the beauty of nature to give perspective to the insignificant problems that can become overwhelming.

Finding expression of this spirit in the way we live and the objects with which we surround ourselves is the common denominator of the country look. It is a look that takes its cue from the irresistible idiosyncracies of country vernacular architecture. It is a celebration of character: the most

obvious difference between town and country building is that in the country, beyond the boundaries of frequent public transport, there are no anonymous copybook terraces. This is no longer the domain of the disturbingly identical suburban villa; from Georgian manor to potting shed, everything has the invincible personality that comes from being purpose-built.

❧ THE COUNTRY MESSAGE ❧

THE KEY WORDS THAT EXPRESS the country look are natural, authentic, fresh, simple and harmonious. If these remind you of some hippie credo, remember that among the wilder notions of those decades, now thankfully obliterated, were some ideas worth keeping. There was a humanity and a tolerant appreciation of originality that were definitely life-enhancing.

The advantage that we have now is being able to look at things in this way but without being weighted down by quasi-religious seriousness. We can concentrate on all the elements that enhance life, editing out all the rest. For example, it is worthwhile, from time to time, to take a room and go through all the objects in it one by one, asking yourself "Does this make me feel good?" It is surprising how many of the unconsidered mainstays of life actually make you feel extremely gloomy — that sofa, for example, bequeathed to you by some well-meaning aunt, may provide a soft perch but it also fills your heart with despair. The ill-considered clutter that creeps into our lives can contribute to muddle within.

The country message is to look afresh at your surroundings, to celebrate the charms and virtues of the things in your home that you love, and to be ruthless with the rest.

The great outdoors (LEFT) *Painted the mutable gray of gathering rain clouds, offset by crisp white window frames, this porch is a pleasantly soothing pause between the wind-blown autumn outside and the warmth of a country kitchen inside the house.*

Sportive corner (LEFT INSET) *Part of the appeal of the country is the accessibility of outdoor pursuits. The window panes of this "Dutch door" or stable door invite a glimpse of the croquet potential of the weather, and strike a nice balance between indoor warmth and outdoor freshness. For less energetic sport, the checkerboard was made by the owner herself in an idle moment.*

CHAPTER ONE

Restoration Drama

A S ANYONE WHO HAS BEEN brave enough to move into an old house knows, the first step towards its restoration is wholesale destruction. Down come the plastic tiles, off comes the woodchip wallpaper (and twenty-two other kinds of wallpaper beneath that), off come the hardboard sheets on the paneled doors, and with them millions of panel pins. Then you have to strip off the layers of paint with which someone has covered the quarry tiles, and, worst of all, you have to try to chisel off the layers of distemper which blur the cornice moldings for which you bought the house in the first place.

Having said this, the transformation of your house from ugly duckling to the kind of home you always used to dream about is ample reward for all the backbreaking work involved. Restoring, decorating and caring for your house can equal the exasperating joy of bringing up small children – and is a source of continual pleasure.

You can make life more bearable by observing a few simple rules. For instance, whatever the state of the house you buy, you must make sure that there is one civilized room almost immediately, and a functioning bathroom and kitchen as soon as possible. And if you assume that you and your builder will loathe each other by the end of the job, you may avoid the trap of employing a friend of a friend, or a man with a good joke repertoire. Your builder can become a terrifyingly important person in your life, so you would be well advised to choose him with care.

Faking with care (LEFT) *This raised pine paneling is a scrupulous recent fake whose conviction comes from using original proportions and color.*

WALLS & CEILINGS

W<small>E ARE BEDEVILLED BY AN</small> anachronistic passion for perfection. There have been times when a faultlessly smooth, flat wall surface represented the triumph of civilization over warfare and chaos. In the 1950s and early 1960s for example, new was good and machine-made was exciting. But now, as we stand amid the trashy debris of those regrettably non-bio-degradable days, there is a nostalgia for particularity and character, and for the enduring methods and artifacts of the past, whose robust practicality improves with time and use. This applies to the fabric of buildings no less than to their contents. Whereas once it was common to disguise bumpy walls by using tongue-and-groove timber, now it is more often used to give personality to flat plaster, particularly if it is given a sympathetic paint finish (see page 84).

Old walls should be treated with respect. Authenticity is the key word, preserving appropriate details – the texture of the walls, the crisp or wobbly finish of corners, the presence or absence of cornice moldings – to confirm the character and period of a building.

Wooden paneling

Wood, in various forms of paneling, almost always makes a sympathetic wall finish. Simple chamfered – or bevelled – paneling, and matchboarding (thin, softwood boarding) impart warmth to a room. They

Painted brick (BELOW) *The solid central pillar of this converted Martello tower is simply painted in functional white, to blend with the pine and stone on the floor and to reflect the masculine strength of the building.*

Graceful aging (RIGHT) *The crisp newness of these extension walls has been softened by timber-cladding. The wood has been stained with gray fabric dye to counteract its natural tendency to go yellow.*

Tudor restoration (FAR RIGHT) *The rough warmth of an original paneled screen wall – much abused by time but now carefully reconstructed – in this early Tudor cottage makes a telling contrast to polished antiques.*

take kindly to color, particularly if you use calm, semi-matte water-based paints with a slight bloom. Dark Jacobean paneling, with its smoky color and hefty linenfold carving, is more oppressive, especially in small rooms, but it provides the perfect setting for somber antique furniture.

Medieval walls

A smooth, mirror-flat surface on walls destroys the character of timber-framed cottages. Rough plaster is not difficult to emulate, if such walls need renovation. First, peel off the Georgian hair plaster carefully with a scraper, exposing the old wattle and daub, clay and dung (which you would be wise to keep very dry – unless you relish the odor of medieval privy). Large holes should be patched with bonding plaster, small ones with filling plaster. Then concoct a custardy slurry with the filling plaster and apply it unevenly with a spatula (see opposite).

The more ancient and humble a building, the less kindly it will take to moldings or wallcoverings. Irregular rooms, and an uneven wall surface is best served by simplicity of treatment, using plain white or thin washes of color, and perhaps traditional stencils for decoration (see page 91).

Eighteenth-century walls

No one but the most confirmed philistine would tamper with the orderly proportions of a Regency or Georgian house, the inspired whimsy of chinoiserie or Gothic revival, or the calm geometry of paneling in an eighteenth-century Connecticut colonial house. These are the models to which less distinguished dwellings can aspire. Some thoughtful research and help from a professional carpenter and cabinet-maker can reproduce some of the more telling elements – walls articulated by regular panels, for example, perhaps also with a paneled and partly glazed built-in corner cupboard.

Towards the end of the eighteenth century wood-paneled rooms were superseded by a combination of plaster and wood. If your house dates from this period, restrict wooden details to a chair rail, skirting, and door and window frames. Molded plaster, in the form of simple cornices, can add further three-dimensional interest.

Victorian precision

If you have a Victorian house, you should remember that the Victorians, with their passion for pattern, wallpapered anything that stayed still for more than five seconds and brought plastering to a fine and precise level of artistry. This is not the place for shaggy, medieval walls.

The Victorian passion for plaster decoration included the ceiling as well as walls. Modern fibrous plaster ceiling roses, cornices and moldings of authentic antique design are easy to come by to replace their missing forebears, and make a huge contribution to the look of a nineteenth-century room.

PLASTER FINISH

THIS TECHNIQUE IS IDEAL IF you have very uneven walls or simply want to keep an authentic look by having a rough-looking finish, rather than careful paintwork or wallpaper. The plaster filler can be applied quite thinly, just enough to create the effect of unevenness. For a soft bloom of color, use the dry-brush technique (see page 78); or perhaps add stencils.

1 *Use an all-purpose filler, spreading it on the wall with a triangular spatula or filling knife. Imitate the uneven finish of old plaster, applying the filler quite thinly in random directions. Leave the filler to dry.*

2 *Apply a base color, using emulsion paint. Work the paint well into the texture of the plaster. Leave this layer of paint to dry thoroughly.*

3 *Dip a fresh brush into white emulsion. Wipe out most of this white paint on waste paper before stroking it across the surface of the plaster finish to tone down the strong base color.*

4 *Keep adding dry-brush layers of white paint until you reach the shade that is right for your room. Applying a mellowing varnish is a final optional stage.*

Adding color and texture (ABOVE)
The base color used on this wall was a deep red, to blend in with the wooden beam. Rich, deep colors, especially primary colors, work well for this technique. The dry-brush white layers highlight the surface texture and make a wonderful dusty bloom. The white paint could be slightly tinted for an even subtler final effect.

VICTORIAN PROPORTIONS

THE VICTORIANS HAD rules for everything, and a regulation room of any pretensions was composed vertically of several levels: baseboard, dado (usually decorated with anaglyphic wallpaper), chair rail, and the upper section of wall – a busy showcase for paintings, picture rail, frieze, and elaborate cornice. Victorian interiors never quite recover from the loss of any of these elements. It is almost certain that someone will have removed some or all of these features, and it is a revelation how these rooms settle back more comfortably once you restore their original proportions.

Vertical dimensions *Restoring the decorative levels in a Victorian room will prevent furniture from looking dwarfed by the tall walls.*

The difficulty lies in judging size and proportion, which can be very deceptive when looked at from the ground – ideally you should take a tape measure with you when you visit a neighbor's house of the same vintage where the moldings are intact.

For those lucky enough to have perfect moldings and cornices, from which the merest sprig is missing due to a clumsy piece of work on the part of the previous owner, there are specialist firms who can make an accurate and affordable forgery (see also page 164 for repairing cornices).

Beamed ceilings

Beams are instantly aging – an entirely modern building can be made to look like an old barn or cowshed conversion, or an ancient French chaumière, by the simple expedient of supporting the ceiling with genuine old beams rescued from some decaying farm building. If done sensitively, with authentic beams and their original structural purpose in mind, such fakery looks fine, and is the perfect nesting place for attractive kitchen paraphernalia.

Decorating beams

Timber-framed cottages with aggressively contrasting black beams and white ceilings are less prevalent than they used to be; one can celebrate the antiquity of a room in less overwhelming fashion, by leaving beams their natural silver-gray shade, or even painting them white, and allowing the sculptural quality of the ceiling to speak of its age. Alternatively, it is possible to go in quite a different direction and emulate certain Gothic churches, where the beams are ornately decorated in rich colors.

Antique beams (RIGHT) *The genuine article – an ancient English cottage – whose hefty oak beams are pitted and runneled by centuries of energetic woodworms. By now the timber has matured to be as hard as iron.*

Sympathetic decoration (RIGHT BELOW) *In this old Norfolk farmhouse the owners eschewed the predictable white walls in favor of bright parsley green. The object above the door is not a medieval musical instrument, but a Provençal prune-dryer – essential for every authentic country kitchen.*

Old and new (LEFT) *Old beams are used here in a building barely one year old, to give a convincing and comforting air of antiquity. The owners' aim was to reproduce an old French farmhouse and their success is due to the simplicity of the design and careful choice of elements. A skeletal basket of corn helps the effect.*

FLOORS OF CHARACTER

 COUNTRY FLOORING LOOKS best when made of good, solid, natural materials. Great wide planks of wood: grayish oak, blonde ash or subdued pine, either tongue-and-groove or bracingly gappy; maple as in some American country houses; chunky square terracotta tiles from Norfolk in England, with all the russet colors of baked clay; smooth brick laid close and loose, or firmly mortared; stone flags – in a host of local variations from slates to limestones – worn to gentle undulations by countless feet. Or you could consider making a marble patchwork floor (in a hall – the effect is somewhat busy for a living room) with offcuts acquired from a monumental mason.

Use rugs if you find stone floors cold - the thicker the better. Old-fashioned rag rugs are ideal (see page 104), and your fine Turkish carpet will benefit from having a non-slip underlay.

Another sympathetic and rather more economical flooring material is linoleum, which used to come in the rich colors and patterns of Turkish carpets, and can still be found these days in dark plain colors and mottled marbled effects in subtle colors.

Hardwood boards *Wych elm* (LEFT) *and brown oak* (RIGHT) *To give them a rich sheen, apply many layers of wax floor polish*

Linoleum *Still available in rich colors and with marble effects*

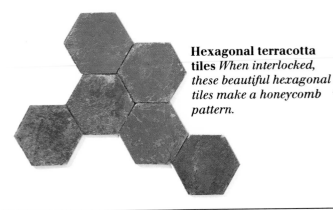

Hexagonal terracotta tiles *When interlocked, these beautiful hexagonal tiles make a honeycomb pattern.*

COUNTRY FLOORS

For a country look, you can't go far wrong with natural materials. Wood has a sympathetic warmth and character that can change or evolve according to your preferences: you can subject a wooden floor to sanding or staining, painting or bleaching. Stone floors and ceramic or quarry tiles need not be cold and they have a convincing air of country dairy about them. They come in rich and subtle colors and are not demanding to care for. Good old lino is a friendly floor-covering – it does not have the repellant, hectic sheen of modern floor-coverings – but it has a tendency to crack in inexpert hands.

Pine boards *Stained with light oak* (LEFT) *and mahogany* (RIGHT)

Oak parquet *New or reclaimed wood block mosaic flooring*

46

Terracotta quarry tiles (ABOVE)

Ceramic floor tile (BELOW, TOP)
*This example has a colorful
design based on an eighteenth-
century wood engraving*

Glazed pavers (BELOW, MIDDLE)
*The thick glaze covers a hand-
molded base*

Unglazed clay tiles (ABOVE) *In various
shapes – octagonal, hexagonal,
rectangle and lozenge.*

**Marble
lozenges** (BELOW)
*Traditionally
laid with white
marble square
inserts*

**Cream-veined
marble** (BELOW)

**Octagonal silver-
blue slate** (BELOW,
TOP) *From East Africa*

**Octagonal
white marble
tile** (BELOW, MIDDLE)

**Green-veined
marble** (BELOW,
BOTTOM)

York stone slab
(ABOVE, TOP)

**Blue english
limestone tile**
(ABOVE, MIDDLE)

**French
limestone flag**
(ABOVE, BOTTOM)

Encaustic tiles (LEFT) *Still made
today, though this example was
found in an architectural
salvage company*

If your house still has its original floors, think hard and long before you change them. Plan any new flooring to match the period and character of your home. Quarry tiles or small bricks add solid authenticity to old cottages; eighteenth-century rooms look best with wooden boards.

Encaustic tiles (which take many stages to make, and are built up rather like *cloisonné* enamel work with different colors of clay being poured into a molded tile) are splendid in Victorian and Edwardian houses, but they will cost almost as much as the house, and suffer from unrepentant newness for a generation or so – they look best when they have been interestingly worn.

Floor with pattern and color
For floors with added color, glazed and patterned ceramic floor tiles come in irresistible designs, and will contribute graceful practicality to kitchens, bathrooms and conservatories.

Bare pine floors can be painstakingly sanded and then, if you love the moiré graining of the wood, you can exploit it with the marvelous soft colors of the new generation of translucent wood stains – foxy russets, gray-greens like a handful of herbs from the Maquis, and brooding storm colors that complement natural wood with beautiful subtlety. You can emulate tiles, or simple geometric patchwork patterns in combinations of different hues. Try one or two coats, and when you like the color, protect it with several layers of clear varnish, preferably satin or matte.

Effects with paint
Painted floors can look fresh and breezy – reminiscent of seaside duck-boarding – and require much less violent exertion than sanding and sealing. They do have to be scrubbed clean, but not necessarily sanded to glassy perfection. Make sure any loose boards are secured. If you have to replace a floor, you can forgo real wood floorboards: hardboard

Stone floor (ABOVE) *A handsome bluestone slab floor adds character to a modern American house. It caused havoc to begin with – the owners painted the stone too thickly with boiled linseed oil and went away for a week, instead of wiping off the excess and wax-polishing a day later. The abandoned oil set like toffee and they had to strip the entire floor.*

Tiled floor (LEFT) *This marvelous mixture of rich natural colors and textures articulates a change in level between half-timbered cottage and extension. Small touches, like laying the tiles diagonally and alternating terracotta with black, make a huge difference to the floor's success.*

Rustic mixture (ABOVE) *A door marks the junction here between pine and terracotta. Polished boards look good butted up against large floor tiles, whose weathered warmth is neatly delineated with dark grouting. The solid door, with its unusual and pretty paneling, adds another harmonizing color in this rich mixture of country materials.*

grooved to look like timber planks and laid on a chipboard foundation can be just as effective once you have painted it with theatrical panache.

For an overall background color either stain the wood (see below) or apply a paint primer and an undercoat. The design itself will need hardwearing eggshell paint or a mix of powder paint and varnish (use matte varnish, if you dislike a shiny finish). If your penchant is for the theatrical, you could paint your floor in great swirls of autumnal colors. For a slightly less dominant look, you could fabricate a harlequin pattern of tiles – dark red and British racing green look good together; or fake a Turkish carpet or a simplified French Aubusson rug in soft colors.

If you want something quicker and easier, simply paint a wide border around the room – a geometric design on a plain ground looks very effective.

For perfect finesse, you could distress the area just inside the door, to make it look footworn, and leave the paint under the window slightly more opaque to look time-bleached. Finally, seal the whole floor with several layers of polyurethane varnish.

Transforming new boards
(RIGHT) *A little artful distressing, wood stain and the rich colors of this stencil design combine to give the impression of an authentic old floor, even though the floorboards are new, inexpensive pine boards.*

STENCILING FLOORS

PAINT BRUSH
STENCIL BRUSH
Distressing tools: SCREWDRIVER, HAMMER, RETRACTABLE KNIFE OR SCALPEL
STAIN & BRUSH
POSTER PAINT
STENCIL PAPER
VARNISH AND BRUSH
READY-MIXED PAINT

S TENCILS ARE THE classic painted floor finish. A repeated all-over design is simple to do and gives a satisfying richness to a room. Pick combinations of colors from old carpets that feel comfortable with the rest of your room and its contents.

Look for, and copy, illustrations of eighteenth-century floors stenciled with seductive irregularity and panache: decorators then considered the floor as a huge canvas to be enjoyed as a whole - with great vigorous borders, strong designs of

wreaths and fan-shapes in the corners or around the edges, and medallions with birds or beasts or heraldic devices in the center of the floor.

For a large choice of color, use powder paint – if possible, first grind it very finely in a pestle and mortar. Mix the powder with varnish. The finished floor will need many layers of clear varnish – with extra layers for areas of hard wear – to protect the paint and allow the floor to be cleaned. Allow at least 24 hours between applying each coat of varnish.

1 *New floorboards need some ruthless treatment before you begin to paint, to make them look old. Use a screwdriver, blades and a hammer to scratch and bruise the wood.*

2 *Apply a stain to the bare boards. Choose a medium-toned color for the stain – nothing too rich or dark which might overwhelm the paint finish. These pine boards are stained with walnut.*

3 *Once you have decided on the pattern for the floor, mark out the area. Find the middle of the area first, with string fastened diagonally across the corners, and draw up reference squares for repeating patterns.*

4 *Mix powder paint with varnish until you have a thick, viscous consistency. Following the guidelines, lay the stencil on the floor and apply the paint with a stencil brush. When dry, apply several protective coats of varnish.*

STAIRWAYS

STAIRWAYS CAN BE DARK, drafty and utilitarian, or they can become an impromptu extension of a sitting room, with a small art gallery thrown in for interest. Stairs from the hall often have a narrow shelf running parallel to the first floor, which can be the perfect place to display a small collection, because it can be seen from several angles.

Wooden stairs are an underexploited showcase for paint and stencil. If you are extremely clever, you can create two paintings – one on the treads to be seen as a whole from above, and one on the risers to be seen as you approach the staircase. If that seems like a lot of work to expend on a stairway, you might consider simply stenciling a line of fake blue and white tiles, or a flower motif, or bold typography on the risers.

In Victorian houses, you may find traces of a long-removed dado rail. Replacing it can be startlingly effective, giving a large, bland area purpose and proportion – the dado rail leads the eye upstairs. For some reason, many Victorian staircases have suffered from a subsequent unruly passion for boxing in the balustrades. Approach this situation with caution, however, because removing the offending hardboard may reveal a complete lack of banisters. All of which can be replaced, but it is a tedious and expensive job.

Another sad loss is the vanishing stair-rod. Besides looking good, stair-rods had distinct advantages over fixed carpets – you could, for example, move the worn carpet on the treads down a few inches, to keep the wear even. It was even possible to remove the carpet if it needed to be repaired.

Bold stairs (ABOVE) *This military building has been converted into an unusual home – a no-nonsense modern stairway, in keeping with the functional character of the tower, has been slung down from the first floor, and makes an appropriate setting for a brooding portrait by Egon Schiele.*

Old and worn (LEFT) *Satin-polished wood makes a handsome staircase. Here its character is enhanced by years of wear and tear and a crudely repaired riser.*

Edwardian gentility (RIGHT) *Light finishes to walls, such as this sugar-pink wash, are kind to solid and simple styles. Here the effect is reinforced by a leavening beam of sunlight coming through a mullioned window on the stairs. The casually placed picture – a Georgia O'Keefe reproduction – adds more interest and color to this corner.*

HEARTHS & STOVES

IN ANY LATITUDE WITH COLD winters, the friendliest part of a house will be near the fireplace. Radiators, lovable though Victorian cast-iron specimens can be, just do not exert the same magnetism, or induce the same languorous torpor. And though these days it seems decadent to have a fire in a bedroom, a century ago there would have been no alternative.

The fireplaces in an old house have often fallen victim to the inexorable march of modernization, so you may be contemplating the tricky question of finding perfect replacements. Inauthenticity really shows, and so do mistakes with proportions. You may fall in love with a high altar of an English Edwardian fireplace, all intricate black and gold. It just might have an unexpected baroque charm in your tiny white-washed cottage, but it is far more likely to sulk, menacing and incongruous. Similarly, you may like the simplicity of that nice old pine surround, only to find it dwarfed by your high-ceilinged sitting-room. Check out successful fireplace transplants in similar houses to your own, and then, within the consequent parameters of size and style, you can explore local architectural salvage yards, bearing in mind that the prices of restored surrounds will leave you weak.

But solving the fireplace surround problem opens a Pandora's box of further worry – unless you find a suitable fireplace complete with its own grate, you now have to make the perfect marriage of grate to surround. Your best guides here are your own taste, your tape-measure and a dealer with experience and a high turnover of fireplace accouterments.

Solid fuel stoves

Stoves are less romantic and more practical than open fires. They can do efficient things like heat domestic water and radiators, and even cook your dinner. They can stand in the middle of a room, and radiate heat in all directions. For a wonderful aroma, try burning apple-wood, or throw in a sprig of rosemary. Swedish, ceramic-clad, wood-burning stoves, like those featured in the paintings of Carl Larsson, are very attractive, and you can find contemporary versions of the cylindrical-shaped French Alsace or Godin stoves, often with pierced-metal decoration.

The versatility of stoves (RIGHT) *Seen through an antique monastery door, a wood-burning American* *"Atlanta" stove dominates this kitchen. It produces food – cooked on its hot plates – as well as warmth.*

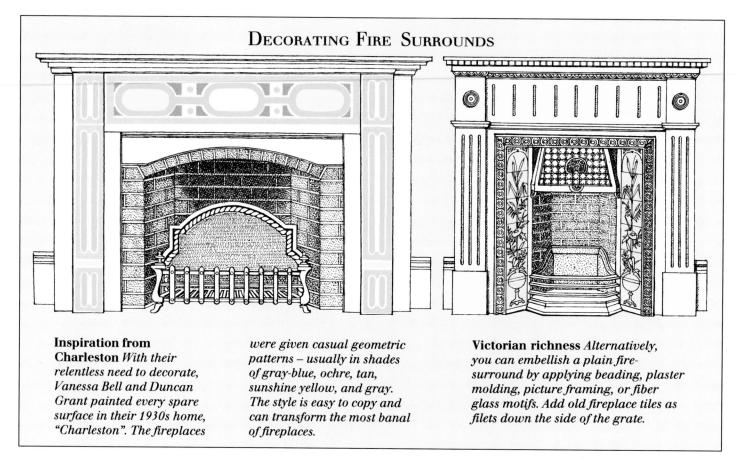

DECORATING FIRE SURROUNDS

Inspiration from Charleston *With their relentless need to decorate, Vanessa Bell and Duncan Grant painted every spare surface in their 1930s home, "Charleston". The fireplaces* *were given casual geometric patterns – usually in shades of gray-blue, ochre, tan, sunshine yellow, and gray. The style is easy to copy and can transform the most banal of fireplaces.*

Victorian richness *Alternatively, you can embellish a plain fire-surround by applying beading, plaster molding, picture framing, or fiber glass motifs. Add old fireplace tiles as filets down the side of the grate.*

Handsome efficiency
(ABOVE) *Utter simplicity and efficiency from Scandinavia – this is a Jøtul wood-burning stove that looks at home against plain painted clapboard walls and scrubbed terracotta tiles.*

Modern stove, traditional look (ABOVE) *Sometimes a modern stove design will work well in a period country setting. This modern multi-fuel English stove from Norfolk has traditional good looks as well as the capability to heat a large dining room very effectively.*

KITCHENS & BATHROOMS

THE PERFECT KITCHEN FORMULA has come about by slow, comforting evolution. It is a recipe that is hard to beat: the room is large and warm, with a huge table in the middle, a slightly undulating quarry-tiled floor, geraniums and a dozing cat on the windowsill, and dressers and shelves full of cook books and old pieces of Mason's ironstone china. There should be plenty of color – on walls, pans, cushions and old containers. Handsome old enamel, wood and metal cooking equipment can be bought cheaply in junk shops and it is effortlessly effective to collect a heap of vaguely matching china to show off. Chips and cracks and broken bits do not matter: a countrified kitchen should look lived in.

This is the place for creative carpentry – to convert old pine cupboards into sink stands, or benignly mutilate a wobbly sideboard to house the boiler discreetly. There is no mystique about a kitchen – built-in furniture is not obligatory. But if you cannot resist the sleek tidiness and regularity of matching units, then simple wooden doors (which can be recycled from other furniture) with brass or ceramic handles, and tiled or wooden worktops (see page 173) have the most countrified air.

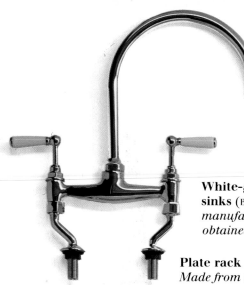

Pillar sink mixer *Here in brass with porcelain lever action, based on a design of 1910*

White-glazed fire-clay sinks (BELOW, TOP) *Still manufactured, or can be obtained secondhand*

Plate rack (BELOW, BOTTOM) *Made from beech wood*

PLUMBING FIXTURES

OF ALL MODERN design, plumbing fixtures seem to have suffered most from a fatal dislocation between purpose and style. Modern tap fixtures tend to be not only violently vulgar, but also impractical; bath tubs and basins are nowadays manufactured in instantly dated colors, in plastics that look scratched within minutes and magnify every smear of soap. Old-fashioned fixtures are both sculptural and practical – the faucets turn when your hands are slippery, and they are relatively easy to dismantle when you need to replace a washer.

Brass faucets and plumbing fixtures are handsome, but they are demanding.

They need constant and tedious polishing, which is why busy people took to chrome with such alacrity. If you can bear to spend your weekends with duster and polish, buffing up your fixtures, then enjoy them. It is often possible to strip down chrome faucets to reveal the brass underneath.

Any antique market will be able to supply you with more splendid brass and chrome fixtures than you will you know what to do with, but bear in mind that genuine antiques may cause problems in installation or be hopelessly stained. Consider instead modern reproductions if you want efficient plumbing as well as good looks.

Handmade tiles *Delicate border designs* (LEFT AND RIGHT) *and Mexican motifs* (CENTER)

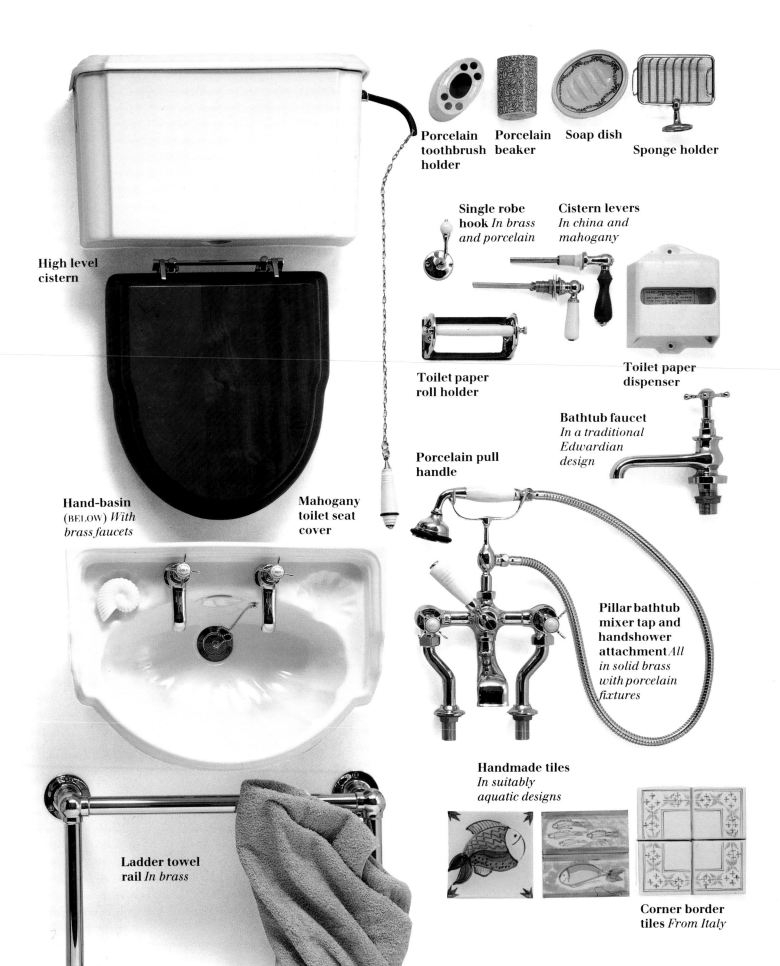

Porcelain toothbrush holder

Porcelain beaker

Soap dish

Sponge holder

High level cistern

Single robe hook *In brass and porcelain*

Cistern levers *In china and mahogany*

Toilet paper roll holder

Toilet paper dispenser

Bathtub faucet *In a traditional Edwardian design*

Porcelain pull handle

Hand-basin (BELOW) *With brass faucets*

Mahogany toilet seat cover

COLD HOT

Pillar bathtub mixer tap and handshower attachment *All in solid brass with porcelain fixtures*

Handmade tiles *In suitably aquatic designs*

Ladder towel rail *In brass*

Corner border tiles *From Italy*

Amid your country clutter you also need to consider the mundane demands of practicality. Unless you want to be a slave to polish and blacking, you will have to forget authenticity and look for the least offensive of the essential modern conveniences. Nicely rounded refrigerators of the pink Chevrolet era can still be found, and have a great deal more charm than their crisp and surgical modern equivalents; but probably no sensible person would want a second-hand fridge. Dishwashers, too, will demand attention with their blinding whiteness; it is possible to mitigate the glossy aggression of these white appliances with stencil and car-spray, but hard and rectangular they will always be.

Compatible kitchenware

The classic country cooker, amenable and sweet-natured if you can get on with it, is the Aga or Rayburn solid fuel stove. Its appeal, and its disadvantages, both lie in the fact that solid fuel cooking requires a distinctly Zen approach to time. Alternatively, industrial cookers are impressively good-looking in a sturdy sort of way, particularly American and French professional stoves.

There is a nostalgic appeal for deep Belfast sinks, made from white glazed earthenware, and old brass mixer taps (with washers so rare that you have to buy in bulk from the manufacturer). A more practical alternative is to go for the unobtrusive. Stainless steel ages better than most and dulls down to pewterish respectability. Always get sinks larger than you think will be necessary. Ideally, have two – so that one can be filled with wilting houseplants, leaving the other free for filling the kettle.

The perfect bathroom

A bathroom can be one of the most pleasurable rooms in a country house. A slant of sun filtered through cotton lace; a large table beneath the window, covered in books and magazines; thick towels warmed by an efficient heated towel rack; and warm matting underfoot – this is the perfect combination of pleasure and puritanism.

If you have the space, the best bathtub of all is a great Victorian bathtub with a wide roll edge. It can stand proudly on ball and claw feet in the middle of a respectably large room, or be boxed in with a shelf all round and paneled.

Painter's kitchen
(LEFT) *A bright, eclectic mixture of different styles and periods can often make a stunning display, as in this kitchen. This capacious crockery cupboard, built with the house in 1902, stores 1930s Fiesta ware and Chinese enamel dishes.*

Chef d'oeuvre (RIGHT) *This professional chef's stove is for serious cooks who have a fastidious eye for good design. It is typical of professional European and American ranges that combine practicality with strong good looks.*

Stylish do-it-yourself
(ABOVE) *An entire house was designed around this kitchen table, which is over 9 feet long. The kitchen cabinets were built of pine and painted dark beige (after a mistaken foray into sky-blue). The counter top is a seamless slab of maple. An ingenious use has been found for the candlerack over the sink – as efficient storage for glasses.*

Ordinary contemporary bathtubs also look best if they are boxed in (see page 167). You could also add a wooden or tiled shelf to fit under the rim of the bathtub on the outside, supported on a battened framework. This is one way to organize all the paraphernalia which collects in bathrooms. The sides of the bathtub can then be paneled, painted, stenciled or tiled, in keeping with the rest of the room.

The best of bathroom design
Basins, toilet bowls and sinks all too often embody the worst of 1960s design without any technical advance over their nineteenth-century ancestors. The toilet bowls of the last century, for example, were objects of real beauty, with sculptural lines, comfortably throne-like mahogany seats, and the ceramic from which they were made was often finely decorated with

inscriptions or flowers. Failing such a paragon, it is still quite easy to get hold of handsome bathroom suites dating from the beginning of the century until the 1930s, when bathroom design lost its way. And if the thought of secondhand bathroom fixtures strikes you as highly dubious, there are excellent reproductions.

Showers can be fitted into the smallest spare corner – under the stairs, just inside the back door, or in a cupboard. Ideally, the shower space should be tiled, with a glazed door and marble floor.

Decorating the bathroom
Tiles are the practical answer for floor, splashbacks and bath surrounds, particularly if you have energetic young children. There is a wonderful range of styles and colours which you can exploit – look for uneven,

New life for an old bath tub (ABOVE) *The inside of this nicely rounded cast-iron bathtub is painted with enamel paint – a successful temporary treatment for a worn enameled bathtub. The basin echoes the Victorian theme with a wooden surround, Victorian tiles for a splashback, and old brass faucets.*

Reviving 1930s elegance (RIGHT) *This bathtub is a magnificent example of 1930s streamlined design. Attention has been paid to appropriate details – the cunning inclusion of the anorexic but sturdy radiator, and strangely anthropomorphic faucets beneath another essential bathroom shelf.*

uneven, glazed, hand-painted tiles or you can make a brilliant patchwork of old, non-matching Victorian tiles. If the room is adequately heated – especially underfloor heating – tiles need not be cold or clinical.

Bathroom walls can be painted with anything other than gloss paint (which exacerbates condensation). Wallpaper gives the room a friendly warmth; protect the area around the bathtub with perspex panels.

For the bathroom floor, cork is warm to the feet and copes well with water. Linoleum is also practical, but for a warmer effect try sisal matting or even a carpet (if you are a tidy bather).

Unless you have small children and need child-proof doors on cupboards, you can eschew ugly modern medicine cabinets, with their obligatory mirror on the front. Look instead for old-fashioned cupboards or shop-fitting cabinets.

Simple grace (ABOVE) *You can still find sanitary ware from the beginning of the century – sold by architectural salvage firms – and enjoy its fuss-free grace. This basin is typical and is both stylish and functional.*

Traditional setting (LEFT) *This room is basically a cupboard put to good use. The walls have been lined with matchboarding and surround a tiny basin that has a marble top and antique taps. The high-level cistern has a traditional wooden housing and a mahogany lavatory seat completes the* fin-de-siècle *picture.*

Neat storage solutions (RIGHT) *A narrow shelf at dado level solves the most urgent of bathroom storage problems neatly and attractively. The simple device of echoing the channels of tongue-and-groove timber with a striped wallpaper is fresh and quietly opulent. The handsome basin came from a junkyard and is now re-fitted with old faucets; the most expensive acquisition here was in fact the little antique French glass lamp.*

LIGHT RELIEF

IT IS SURPRISING HOW MANY otherwise successful country homes are let down by
insensitive lighting. Central light fixtures
are a disaster, casting either the blinding
brightness of an operating theater, or
sepulchral gloom. The answer is to create intimate
areas of light with table lamps and standard lamps, or
even with candles.

Kindly lights

Victorian lamps, silk-shaded, cast a kindly light over a
table. The Victorians excelled in manipulating light –
for instance, they might exaggerate the gloom of an
entrance hall by painting it maroon or indigo, in order
to create more contrast with the parlor, with its big
bay windows radiating sunlight. And at night, table
lamps made small friendly areas of interest within the
dark, heavily draped rooms.

Brass angle lamps – antique or reproduction – with
green glass shades are friendly to work by, and simple
wooden candlestick lamps with beautifully painted or
lacquered bases have the advantage of taking up very
little room and look very pretty with classic dark gold-
banded or pleated paper shades.

Paraffin lamps shed a friendly light, and old ones
are beautiful objects in their own right. They never
recover from being converted to electricity –
candlelight bulbs are never convincing, although if
you fit frosted glass globes you can blur their too-
precise brilliance.

Pendant light fittings, with glass, metal or fabric
shades and an antiquated rise-and-fall mechanism
cast inviting pools of light over a table – the trouble is
that if they are low enough not to blind you, they are
also low enough effectively to obliterate the person
sitting opposite you.

LIGHT FIXTURES

MODERN LIGHTING gets
bigger and brighter,
but it does not necessarily
get any better; one could
say that we are in the dark
ages as regards lighting.
Very few contemporary
light fixtures are things of
beauty – those that look
good, and cast a friendly
beam, tend to be based on
turn-of-the-century
precedent. In general,
strategic small sources of
light are more sympathetic
than bright central fixtures,
though frosted-glass bowl-
shaped diffusers hanging
from chains can shed an
inoffensive overall
radiance, when partnered
by graceful ceramic table
lamps or delicate painted
candlestick lamps. As usual,
simplicity fits best with a
country ethos: a flotilla of
candles, perhaps set out in
spidery-black candle-
holders or tin sconces,
creates the perfect
atmosphere for good
conversation.

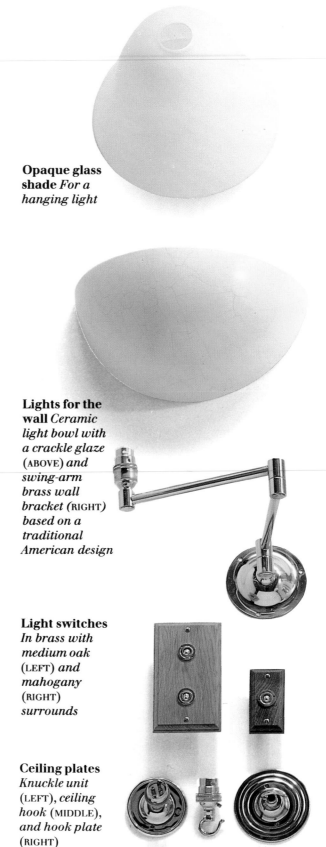

**Opaque glass
shade** *For a
hanging light*

**Lights for the
wall** *Ceramic
light bowl with
a crackle glaze
(*ABOVE*) and
swing-arm
brass wall
bracket (*RIGHT*)
based on a
traditional
American design*

Light switches
*In brass with
medium oak
(*LEFT*) and
mahogany
(*RIGHT*)
surrounds*

Ceiling plates
*Knuckle unit
(*LEFT*), ceiling
hook (*MIDDLE*),
and hook plate
(*RIGHT*)*

Rise and fall pendant lamp *With counterweight*

Painted tin candlestick lamp bases *Requiring the simplest of shades*

Georgian wooden candlestick lamp base

Trough lamp *Traditional turn-of-the-century design for a desk lamp*

Traditional candlestick lamp bases *In brass* (LEFT), *and mahogany* (RIGHT)

Pastiche lamp *Unusual use of découpage inside the glass base to give an effect like Chinese lacquer*

Tin candle sconce (BELOW) *Reflects the light of the candle and protects the flame from drafts*

Wooden lamp base *With a sponged paint finish*

Paraffin lamps *Can be found in antique shops or as modern reproductions, as well as in hardware shops*

Kashmiri candlestick (ABOVE LEFT) **Handmade decorated earthenware candlestick** (RIGHT)

65

In the kitchen you need light on specific areas. Directional spotlighting is harsh and ugly, and fluorescent tube lighting is hideous, except possibly at low levels beneath hanging cupboards and over worktops where the light source itself can be hidden. There is no reason why, in the kitchen as elsewhere, the room should not be lit in small areas, with a soft overall illumination from ceramic uplighters which can be painted to blend with the rest of the room.

Making your own bases and shades
Table lamps provide numerous possibilities for ingenious bases and shades. Big ceramic bases have a nostalgic appeal in grayish-green celadon glaze, or crackle-glaze. Once upon a time country house owners had a perfectly unselfconscious talent for converting large chinese tea canisters and porcelain statuettes and vases into handsome lamp bases – even big, glass sweet jars filled with a decorative ballast of seashells. But this approach has to be treated with extreme caution and vigilance to avoid the slightest hint of Chianti bottledom.

If you are feeling creative, painted paper shades in 1930s colors are not difficult to imitate, and glow like stained glass. Homemade shades have to be done well in order not to look folksy, but they are an under-exploited area for showing off fabrics and papers. The simple expedient of punching thick craft paper finely in flower or geometric designs can produce an effect as pretty as frozen fireworks.

For convenience, have all your table lamps wired to a single switch, because turning off a dozen awkwardly-placed lamps can be very tedious last thing at night.

Massed candle-power
(LEFT) *Reproduction candelabra with simple Shaker elegance are easy to come by in America. They require a certain energy and dedication – the candles have to be frequently replaced, and their light is a disaster for close work. Impractical as they are, they have a graceful charm; your other light fixtures can be sensible.*

Solo candlelight (RIGHT)
Tin candle sconces give a muted reflection of candlelight. Easily made out of the cheapest and most freely available material, original and reproduction sconces are to be found in many antique shops. They often have heart motifs or simple punched decoration.

Sweetness and light
(ABOVE) *Lighting does not
have to be too earnest – as
long as there is a sensible
light source somewhere by
which to work or read, the
rest can be no more
practical then illuminated
artworks. This boy eternally
scrutinizing his globe just
adds a touch of warmth and
whimsy to a dark corner.
The lampshade beneath was
a simple unadorned shop-
bought shade, painted
freehand by the owner, so
that it glows like stained
glass when the lamp is lit.*

DOORS & WINDOWS

YOUR FRONT DOOR leaves a lasting impression – it is the first and last thing people see of your house; the door itself may become something of a symbol of the way you live and your aspirations.

The classic, unpretentious country door has narrow tongue-and-groove with cross-bracing. Elizabethan doors from just two widths of tongue-and-groove timber are handsome, but hard to find or fabricate.

Classic paneled doors

There is nothing to beat the classic proportions of paneled doors. They come in thousands of different permutations – from a simple double panel, to ornate double doors with ten panels between them, which can be further embellished by carving or marquetry. The proportions of the panels varied from one era to the next: the Jacobeans often favored small square panels; early eighteenth-century doors had beveled round-headed and cross-braced panels; later in the eighteenth century panels on doors were both vertical and horizontal.

Paneled outside doors look good painted black or red or a good strong dark green – military colors that go well with brass door furniture. Back doors, on the other hand, look fine in the cracked and faded blues and greens of French farmhouse doors.

Stained glass and plain glazed panels, in the door itself, or in the transom light above it – particularly in etched or strong Victorian red and blue glass – are a useful light source in a dark hall, and shed a lovely precise beam of light when the sun shines through them. The patterns on contemporary glass are often ugly – better to find stained glass panels, or have them made, or use plain or etched frosted glass.

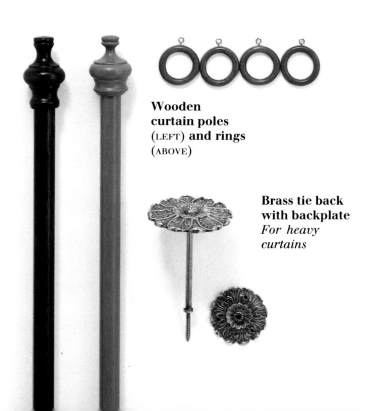

Brass window latch

Sliding casement stay

Matte black iron casement stay

Brass casement stay and quadrant stays

Details for blinds *Wooden acorn, brass cord knob, brass cleat-hook, and antique blind pull*

DOOR AND WINDOW DETAILS

DOOR FURNITURE – hinges, locks, handles, latches, knockers, escutcheons and finger plates – repays diligent research. There are excellent reproductions available of all periods and they can make a huge difference to a sense of authenticity. The same applies to windows, where fittings should be in keeping with the period of the rest of the house.

The choice of door and window fittings must be dictated by the personality of your house – heavy oak doors with panels and studs and gnarled black hinges and latches belong to a Tudor mansion (but must be authentic – this is a disaster area for fakes); humble reinforced battened doors (ledged and braced) are right in a cottage; unglazed paneling is right for Georgian houses, and glazed for Victorian. With Georgian houses in particular you should be punctilious about details: slight errors will show.

Wooden curtain poles (LEFT) **and rings** (ABOVE)

Brass tie back with backplate *For heavy curtains*

Hinges *Matte black iron door hinges and brass door hinge*

Leaded light (RIGHT)
Found by an architectural salvage company

Antique painted glass door panel (ABOVE)

Door handles *Matte black iron* (LEFT) *and brass* (RIGHT)

Door knobs *Pair of period wood and brass knobs, modern knobs in porcelain* (TOP) *and brass* (BOTTOM), *antique brass and porcelain knob* (MIDDLE)

Wooden window shutter

Door furniture *Black finger plate, brass loop handle, enamel door number, ceramic and brass escutcheons, and cabin hook fastening*

French window sliding bolt

Finding attractive doors to fit an existing door frame is an easy, if exasperating task. There are countless secondhand and stripped-door merchants, but it will astonish you how many tiny and crucial variations in size and thickness of doors there are. You may find it easiest to start by choosing the doors and then ask the builder to build the opening to fit.

If you want to put in a new door where none existed before, or make a larger door frame, keep a sensitive eye on the period and proportions of the house – it is a good idea to make a scale drawing of the wall and doors first. Altering a door frame is surprisingly straightforward when done by a competent builder (check with an architect or knowledgeable builder about the necessity for a rolled-steel joist).

Countrified windows
Windows give the character to a house, just as features suggest the personality in a face. Small changes in style, finish or proportions of windows can destroy the spirit of your home – consider carefully the effect that changes will make to the outside as well as the inside of the building.

Until the seventeenth century, most windows were of the four-panel casement type, opening outwards (or inwards) like a door on butt hinges. The particular irregularity of the glass is important, and such windows are ruined by insensitive and mechanical metal casements and phoney leaded lights. Thereafter, sash windows became more common in Britain and America; usually they open vertically, but horizontal-sliding sash windows have a peculiar charm and work well in wide, low frames.

Today, we are used to great expanses of glass, but originally windows were busily divided by mullions. The fine art of fenestration seems to have fallen by the wayside – proper leaded lights, decorative Georgian fan-lights, and the dignified proportions conveyed by a satisfying geometry of wooden mullions – seem to be a thing of the past.

DECORATING DOORS

A FLAT, MODERN DOOR can look blank and uninspiring – best approached as a creative challenge. A classical paneled door can be faked using molding, attached with glue and panel pins. You can embellish this further by picking out the panels with paint, or applying fabric or paper to the door and lacquering it when dry. Or you could paint freehand patterns on your simple door, like these exuberantly baroque Florentine fake hinges.

PANELED DOOR   FABRIC-COVERED DOOR   FLORENTINE DOOR

Outside inside (ABOVE) *An attractively complex antique external door – one of an English collection bought in Suffolk – is put to service here inside this house, standing between the entrance lobby and kitchen.*

Barring the way (LEFT) *A late nineteenth-century arts and crafts clock stands sentinel beside a fearsome looking back door. The complicated web of iron struts on the door serves no other function than pure decoration, although the black hinges, bar and bolt all perform in authentic fashion.*

Cottage door (ABOVE) *This hefty external door of a half-timbered cottage, timbers pockmarked by nails, is diagonally braced to prevent the wood sagging. A discreet contemporary deadlock has been added to give more security than the impressive Elizabethan wrought iron latch.*

Replacing old windows with modern versions is almost always to the detriment of a house. Unfortunately, almost all double-glazing is hideous and metal-framed windows are heinous – terrible crimes are committed in the cause of fuss-free windows. And blocking in a window or a glazed door can have a quite disproportionate effect on the light within – look closely at the path of light shed by the glazing in question before you decide to remove it.

Window dressing

The replacement of internal shutters alters the character of a window totally, but second-hand shutters are extremely difficult to fit successfully, particularly to bay windows. Wooden louver blinds give equal privacy in a timeless and inoffensive way, unmatched by anything in plastic.

Where you have two tall windows flanking a fireplace, you could imitate the charming early nineteenth-century style known as Empire, using curtain poles with exuberantly florid knobs, over which a heavy damask curtain is folded and draped in an impressive swag to one side. Add a rectangle of paneling beneath, a mahogany velvet-covered stool, and you have created the perfect setting for a demure Jane Austen heroine.

For a simpler effect – in bathrooms especially – cover windows with a sweep of lace curtain for privacy, or explore the possibilities of stained glass.

Restoring original windows (ABOVE) *These oak mullions were lovingly reconstructed from clues left by the ancient triangular peg holes. The window had been blocked up and hidden for years behind 15 layers of wallpaper.*

Shutters for privacy (RIGHT) *Hand-colored leaded glass in Gothic shutters: a neat and easy way to gain privacy without hiding a handsome new window.*

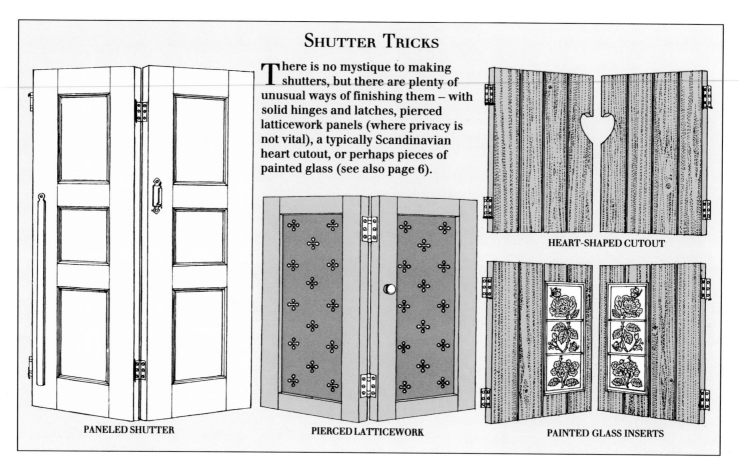

SHUTTER TRICKS

There is no mystique to making shutters, but there are plenty of unusual ways of finishing them – with solid hinges and latches, pierced latticework panels (where privacy is not vital), a typically Scandinavian heart cutout, or perhaps pieces of painted glass (see also page 6).

PANELED SHUTTER

PIERCED LATTICEWORK

HEART-SHAPED CUTOUT

PAINTED GLASS INSERTS

CHAPTER TWO

Decorative Finishes

THERE MAY COME A DAY WHEN a fit of creativity comes upon you; you look around your home and think that just possibly white paint with a hint of apricot is not only safe and inoffensive, it is also dull. You may suddenly realize you want more out of your interior decoration: colors and textures that play up the essential character of each room and help to create the air of the country.

Once you commit yourself to redecoration, turn the house upside-down and start to paint, you will probably think you have never seen anything quite so awful. But however much your heart sinks, you must not jettison your new colors until you have completed the last dab, put the furniture back and returned your pictures to the walls. Even then, it is not a bad idea to live with your efforts for a while, because they will probably grow on you.

One of the best things about paint effects is that you can cover them up or add another warming or diluting layer of paint very quickly. And possibly, if you analyze the effect narrowly, you may come to the conclusion that the color is fine, it just needs definition by adding a stenciled border or *trompe l'oeil* painted paneling, or making a slight adjustment to the existing lighting.

But this is to look on the pessimistic side. Usually, the transformation of a room will be an exhilarating revelation.

Simple techniques for Italianate splendor (LEFT) *An impressive wreath of laurel leaves is made from a simple collage and echoed by a flurry of stenciled leaves on roughly plastered, colorwashed walls. A mellowing varnish was applied across the whole surface to give added protection.*

PREPARING THE SURFACES

TO START WITH, THE ADVICE to make your heart sink: begin by preparing the surface for paint. This is a tedious job, but an essential one too, unless you want your glorious paint finishes to peel off.

Grit your teeth, put on your oldest clothes, and collect all the necessary tools. On walls you may have to remove a thick crust of old wallpaper, fill holes, soak off old paint and sand to an acceptable smoothness. If the existing wall is sound, or neatly finished with a smooth paper which can easily be painted over, then just wash down the surface with sugar soap (cautiously over existing paper), rinse and allow to dry. Sand down woodwork and apply undercoat or emulsion for an even finish beneath oil-based paint.

Applying base coats

If you are planning to decorate your walls with any of the techniques in this chapter, you must give the fancy work a good surface. Most of the techniques that follow will cooperate happily with a couple of flat, even coats of matte or silk emulsion. Choose your base color to harmonize with the scheme you have in mind. A paler shade of whatever is going on top is the safest choice; as you gain confidence with color, you can experiment with contrasts.

Starting to paint

Start with the ceiling, above the windows. Then work your way down the walls, leaving the woodwork until last. Clean up paint drips before they have dried (except for paint that has run on to the glass from window frames – this is easiest to remove with a razor edge when the paint is dry). Water-based paints dry quite quickly, so try to keep a wet edge to receive the fresh paint.

DECORATIVE MATERIALS

IF YOU ENJOY decorating at all, your heart will beat faster in the paint and brushes section of your local DIY shop. There is something about painting tackle that is apt to lure the innocent browser with promise of color and texture and seductive transformations. There is recollection of childish pleasures to be had in mixing paints and poring over books for potential stencil designs. Prices can vary enormously, especially for more specialized artists' colors, but consider mixing your own colors, following instructions in decorators' manuals. There is nothing to lose but your inhibitions.

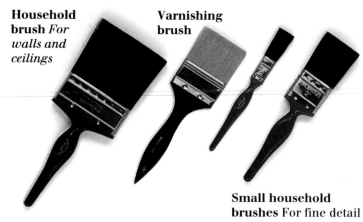

Household brush *For walls and ceilings*

Varnishing brush

Small household brushes *For fine detail*

Smoothing/roughening/aging
Fine sandpaper (BENEATH), *medium sandpaper* (MIDDLE) *and rough sandpaper* (TOP); *with cork sandpaper and hard sander blocks*

Yacht varnish (BELOW, RIGHT) *Particularly hardwearing and excellent for floors*

Turpentine

Art paper (BELOW, TOP) *High quality paper, ideal for drawing designs*

Acetate pad (BELOW, BOTTOM) *Transparent film for stencils; it makes registering colors easier than with manila paper*

Cutting mat (BELOW) *Marked in squares to help accurate cutting*

Retractable modeling knife (BELOW, LEFT)

Craft knives (BELOW, RIGHT)

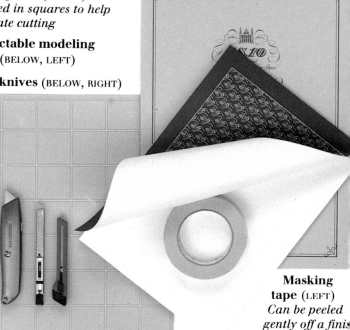

Masking tape (LEFT) *Can be peeled gently off a finish without damaging the paintwork*

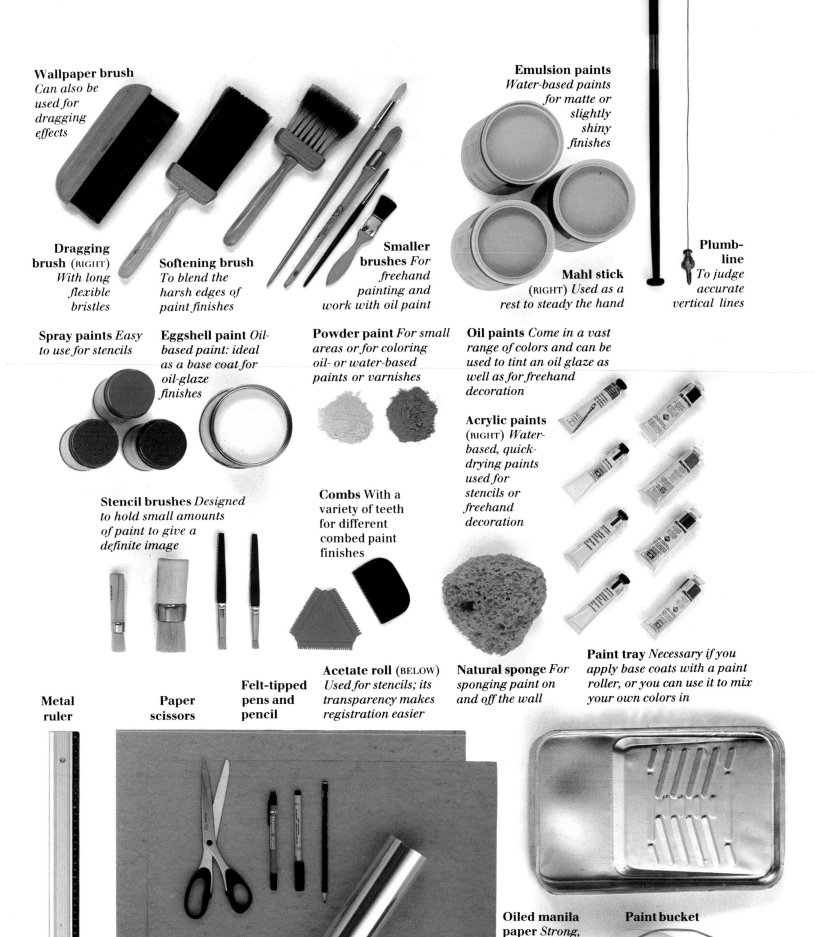

Wallpaper brush *Can also be used for dragging effects*

Dragging brush (RIGHT) *With long flexible bristles*

Softening brush *To blend the harsh edges of paint finishes*

Smaller brushes *For freehand painting and work with oil paint*

Emulsion paints *Water-based paints for matte or slightly shiny finishes*

Mahl stick (RIGHT) *Used as a rest to steady the hand*

Plumb-line *To judge accurate vertical lines*

Spray paints *Easy to use for stencils*

Eggshell paint *Oil-based paint: ideal as a base coat for oil-glaze finishes*

Powder paint *For small areas or for coloring oil- or water-based paints or varnishes*

Oil paints *Come in a vast range of colors and can be used to tint an oil glaze as well as for freehand decoration*

Acrylic paints (RIGHT) *Water-based, quick-drying paints used for stencils or freehand decoration*

Stencil brushes *Designed to hold small amounts of paint to give a definite image*

Combs With a variety of teeth for different combed paint finishes

Metal ruler

Paper scissors

Felt-tipped pens and pencil

Acetate roll (BELOW) *Used for stencils; its transparency makes registration easier*

Natural sponge *For sponging paint on and off the wall*

Paint tray *Necessary if you apply base coats with a paint roller, or you can use it to mix your own colors in*

Oiled manila paper *Strong, non-absorbent paper used for stencil motifs*

Paint bucket

BASIC PAINT TECHNIQUES

I F YOU WANT A GENTLE WASH of color on walls, perhaps as the background for more elaborate decorative techniques, or simply as a soft overall color that will set off the features and furnishings of a room, consider alternatives to plain emulsion paint. One of the quickest effects to achieve is colorwashing – especially suitable for elderly country walls that have a rough and uneven finish.

Colorwashing

Colorwashing produces a patchy, painterly finish of luminous transparency. Use matte or silk-vinyl emulsion (matte has a soft bloom to it, silk is more translucent) in your chosen top color, thinning the paint with water until it is the consistency of thin cream. Brush it quickly and roughly in a random crisscross pattern on to your emulsion base coat. Let it dry, then go through the same procedure with another layer of thinned paint. As you cover the previous layer, harsh lines and jerky patches will soften and blur to a quietly lively texture.

For variety, you can paint layers in different but friendly colors, or tones of the same color. Alternatively, you can experiment with dry-brushing – dip your brush into undiluted paint and brush out most of the paint on waste paper. Then skim the brush in random but even strokes over the preceding color to give a finish slightly reminiscent of the texture of hammered pewter.

A contemplative corner
(LEFT) *The right paint finish will emphasize the features and character of a room. The walls and tent-shaped ceiling of this bedroom are highlighted with color: first they were streaked with peach and gray, and then a magnolia wash was added to dilute the effect. The shutters were created by the owner to cast an ecclesiastical brilliance over the lectern and to give privacy at night without cluttering the lovely shape of the window.*

Simulating sunshine
(RIGHT) *The amount of sunlight that can penetrate a room is an important factor in your choice of color: colors that look wonderful in the Mediterranean sun will probably appear harsh in rooms with cold, northern light. Using soft colors can be the answer: this room has a warm, summer look – whatever the weather is doing outside. The walls and ceiling are colorwashed with burnt umber over white, and topped with a white glaze to soften the overall effect.*

If this effect is startling at close quarters, you can homogenize the layers with a final coat of transparent glaze made from a toning oil-based paint, thinned with turpentine. Or use a ready-made scumble glaze, adding color with a little artists' oil paint.

Ragging and rag-rolling

For a soft, dappled finish, ragging is a very easy technique. Brush a glaze coat of oil-based eggshell paint, thinned with an equal amount of turpentine, over the base color. Then lift off the glaze with a soft cloth. Alternatively, crumple up a rag and roll it up and down the wall. The final effect makes a sympathetic basis for further decorative finishes.

Combing

Combing is a dramatic and simple paint technique that can be used to glorify walls, floors, picture frames and furniture. It is basically a ribbed or striped combination of two colors, created by scraping the teeth of a decorator's comb through a surface glaze. The effect can be as quiet or contrasty as you like.

The combing technique

The surface to be combed should have a smooth finish – gloss, eggshell or varnished emulsion. Then slightly thin your oil-based eggshell top coat with turpentine and mix thoroughly – or use a glaze tinted with a little artists' oil paint – and paint on evenly.

The combs can be regular wide-toothed or Afro combs, or the combs sold for applying adhesive. You can also make your own combs from a length of flexible plastic or a rubber window-washer, in which you cut saw-tooth notches, as fine or as coarse as you like. Or you can butcher a wide, elderly, stiff paintbrush with notches for a softer effect. For little jobs you can use card, but it becomes soggy too quickly for most uses.

Emphasizing details (LEFT) *Combing emphasizes the linear pattern of this paneling. The whole room was given a cool green base, then a glaze tinted with Venetian red oil paint was applied* *and combed off in two directions. The result is rich and moody, adding color and texture to the bare wood.*

New life for old furniture (ABOVE) *An exuberant paint finish will give a new lease of life to tired pieces of furniture. This battered chest of drawers has gained dignity from its subtle moiré of care-* *ful combing. It was initially painted flat cream, over which a layer of yellow became a background for a transparent green glaze.*

Mask off areas with masking tape, if you want firmly-defined edges, or want to confine your pattern within precise boundaries – hardboard floor tiles, for example. Run your chosen comb smoothly and evenly through the wet paint, keeping your stripes as parallel as possible. It helps to confine your attention to one, small, clearly defined area at a time. Finally, seal areas that are to be subject to hard use with varnish.

Dragging
For a variant on combing, dragging can be very effective, although it needs careful practice and a steady hand. Apply a base color and let it dry before brushing on a slow-drying oil-based glaze in a second color. Then drag a clean brush down the wall to create a delicate stripe effect and show the underlying layer of paint. This is an effective way of enlivening a small and neatly organized area, such as a paneled door (see page 83) or shutters.

Sponging
Sponging is a finish to appeal to even the most faint-hearted and paint-shy. It is simple to do and produces a soft cloudy effect with colors that blur gently into each other. It has a kindly cosmetic effect on old walls that are less than perfectly smooth, and you can sponge obtrusive radiators into near-invisibility.

The base coat can be emulsion, which will absorb some of the top colors and give a more muted finish, or a mid-sheen or matte oil-based paint. Add the top coat – one or two, or more if you feel like it – in different toning colors. They can be, in order of transparency, tinted oil-based glaze through which the previous coats will be hazily visible: oil-based mid-sheen paint thinned with the appropriate solvent; or emulsion diluted with water, which gives a soft effect but is not transparent.

How to sponge
If possible, use a natural sponge that gives a casual effect because of its unevenly sized holes. Natural sponges are expensive, but an old, clean sponge will work just as well as a brand new one. If you are using oil-based paint, wring the sponge out in turpentine to soften it; use water if you are working with emulsion. In either case, squeeze out as much moisture as possible, or your paint will be diluted.

Pour your paint into a paint tray, dip the broadest side of your sponge into it, and try the effect, dabbing on to a piece of waste paper. The only delicate judgement is the amount of paint to load on to the sponge so that it leaves an even and light impression without blobs or runs. If you are using two or more colors your sponge marks should be quite widely but

Versatile sponging (RIGHT)
A simple broken paint effect, such as sponging, is as versatile as you could wish. This wall was painted sky blue, with sunset colors sponged on to give a touch of warmth. The color scheme evolved as the painting went along – one of the charms of this kind of paint treatment is the relaxed attitude you can have to color. It is a good idea to experiment on a piece of hardboard first, so that you can see the effect and limber up to the stage where you are enjoying the creative process.

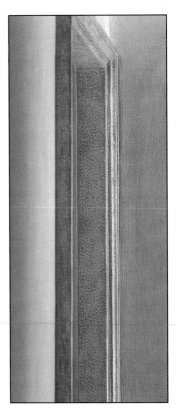

Highlighting techniques (ABOVE) *Techniques like sponging, or the more formal finish of stippling seen here, are as effective on small areas as on a whole wall. Since you can use either water-based paints or oil-based glazes, you can use the same technique for walls or wood, highlighting frames round doors or windows.*

Mixing it (LEFT) *A combination of dragging and sponging gives a visual lift to the features of this paneled door: the main part of the door has been dragged, while the panels were sponged. The informality of the sunny paint finishes suits the curiously uneven lines of the door. The colors have been kept to a similar tone range so that no heavy or dense color jumps out.*

evenly spaced, leaving a good proportion of the background color visible. If you are sponging with a single color you will be able to judge the texture as you go – you can always come back at a later stage to even up any patches.

From time to time you will need to clean the sponge when it gets lumpy and clogged with paint – just wring it out again in water or turpentine as before. If the surface of your sponge begins to disintegrate, slice it back to an undamaged layer and continue with that.

Stippling

Stippling is a pointilliste paint effect, similar to, but finer than sponging. It is done in the same way, using the same kinds of paint, but the paint is applied with a special brush to deposit speckles of color. Because the finish has to be evenly applied with a somewhat mechanical rectangle of stiff bristles, it is trickier than the soft clouds of color produced by sponging.

Traditional blue-green

A soothing treatment for paneled walls and wooden floors, a blue-green colorwash was a frequent element of nineteenth-century painted interiors. It had counterparts in America, Scandinavia and the Regency Green of English country houses, so if it suits your home, you will be following in a strong tradition.

The wash was originally mixed *in situ* by itinerant painters whose repertoire of materials included the earth pigment *terra verde* (green earth), which is the heart of the traditional blue-green tone, and was mixed with egg white and buttermilk.

TRADITIONAL BLUE-GREEN

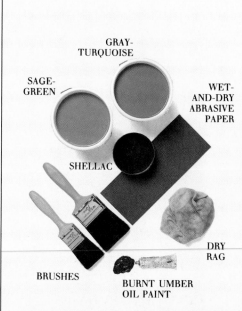

GRAY-TURQUOISE

SAGE-GREEN

WET-AND-DRY ABRASIVE PAPER

SHELLAC

DRY RAG

BRUSHES

BURNT UMBER OIL PAINT

Ύου CAN RECREATE the soothing charm of the blue-green finish without using the original ingredients. The interpretation of traditional blue-green shown opposite is achieved by using straightforward oil-based, satin-finish paints. Choose two tones that approximate the desired color. Smooth bare wood first, to remove any major imperfections that will impair the finish. Using shellac to seal and prime the bare wood avoids an oil-based wood primer that would show white or pink under the paint coats. The shellac allows instead the wood color to show through as the colored paint coats are carefully rubbed back. Applying a clear, satin-finish varnish is an optional final stage.

1 *Apply shellac (diluted with two parts meths) to the bare wood, using a household-quality brush. Leave this to dry.*

2 *Using a good quality brush, apply a layer of blue patchily. After drying, paint an even, flat coat of green on top.*

3 *When the paint is dry, rub it back gently using damp wet-and-dry paper, to reveal blue through green, and hints of grain.*

4 *When the surface is wiped and dry, mix one part burnt umber oil paint with ten parts white spirit. Brush on and wipe off.*

Re-creating a period feel (ABOVE)
These new tongue-and-groove boards, complete with a little shelf, have been cleverly painted in two related tones of modern paint, chosen to approximate

traditional blue-green. A little false aging completes a look that is convincingly close to the genuine article, and a perfect backdrop for country bits and pieces.

DECORATIVE TECHNIQUES

ONCE YOU HAVE A BASE of color on the wall – whether the finish has the translucency of colorwashing or perhaps a textured effect – you can highlight areas of a room with decorative finishes. Before the advent of modern plasters and techniques that produce mirror-flat walls, and mass-produced wallpaper, there were limited ways to achieve an even, figured decoration on large areas. One possibility was to use paint, either applied freehand, or with stencils or blocks. Other decorative effects could be achieved from variants on the techniques of *découpage* – particularly effective if used in a border.

Don't despise these techniques today – used with care they add delicate touches of interest and color. Modern wallpapers may be easier to apply, but these techniques may be more in keeping with the age and character of your home.

Paper cutouts

Paper cutouts are perfect as decorative punctuation for borders, door and shutter panels, drawer fronts and anything that can take a small repeated pattern.

It is a tradition that perhaps originated in Ireland, in the grand Fermanagh home of Lady Louisa Lennox, who applied decorative prints directly to the wall in a manner both formal and whimsical, complete with decorative cutout swags and frames. She used carefully arranged monochrome prints – including portraits; you can copy her ideas, or create your own compositions of cornucopias, cherubs and two-dimensional puns on three-dimensional objects, such as door handles and moldings. The effect can be as light and airy as you wish – try using motifs from wrapping paper, set off by a plain, pale background.

The tradition of stenciling

The word "stencil" is thought to have come from an old French verb meaning to scatter with stars – in the thirteenth century there was a vogue for dark-painted

Decorating with paper and paint (RIGHT) *To provide a sympathetic background to the cutouts used here, the wall was first painted with blue emulsion. A white wash – diluted white paint – was added with random brush strokes for a translucent effect.*

CUTOUTS

MARBLED PAPER

RULER

PENCILS

WALLPAPER PASTE

SCISSORS

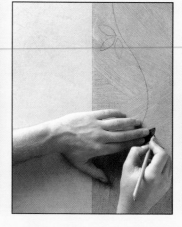

USING CUTOUTS on a wall, especially on a border, is a very easy and effective way to highlight color and create a sophisticated look. You can use wallpaper – and the range is endless – or choose from a variety of wrapping papers. The paper used here is a marbled paper, which is available at specialist shops.

1 *Mark out the paper first. A curved shape like this one need only be drawn once because you can echo the other curved shapes beside it as you cut. Use a sharp scalpel to cut, on top of an old board or piece of thick card.*

2 *Mark out points on the wall with a pencil, as a guide for where the pattern will fall. Measure the distances with a ruler if necessary. A regular pattern can look especially effective inside a border that runs along the bottom of the wall or round a door frame – see opposite for preparing borders.*

3 *Stick down the cutouts with wallpaper paste, following the marks on the wall. If you are creating a border, add a different feature at the corners – as on the wall opposite.*

PAINTING BORDERS

1 (ABOVE) *Mark up the border area with pencil lines (using a plumb line as a guide), then mask off with masking tape.*

2 (RIGHT) *Apply layers of whitewash over the background color, using random brush strokes.*

walls sparkling with gold stars. Medieval journeyman stencilers used to travel the country with a bag full of designs, and would move on when their practiced art had transformed a room with leaves and tendrils, or stripes and stylized flowers.

Even after the evolution of printed wallpaper in the seventeenth century, stenciling remained popular as the poor man's decoration; it became fashionable among the rich again once wallpaper became cheap and freely available in the mid-nineteenth century, acquiring cachet because of its relative expense.

Stencil paints
The colors that were used originally were made from a mixture of powder paint and buttermilk, which gave a clear, pure, flat color. You can copy this effect, mixing the paint with a little fungicide, but you will need to seal it with varnish, if you want the pattern to be permanent, and you will have to remove it completely if you ever want to overpaint it. Or you can use modern, fuss-free paints (including spray paints) for a convenient, if less authentic, finish.

Stencil designs
Stencils are perfect for creating a repeated design, although precise uniformity is not essential to their charm. They can be used for furniture, walls, floors and fabric, and designs can range from the tiniest regular punched background motif to great extrovert swags and swirls as a border on a painted floor. Much of the attraction of early work comes from its broken and distressed color and the background sprinkling of tiny motifs that break up large areas of flat color and outline larger elements in the design.

REVERSE STENCILING

STENCILS CAN WORK extremely effectively as templates. Begin by deciding the color you want the stencil image to be, painting the whole wall that color – here it is plain white. Then cut your chosen shapes in batches from lining paper and stick on to the painted surface. Use spray adhesive, so that the shapes can be removed easily later. Apply a thick wash of emulsion over everything. Once that is dry, carefully peel off the shapes.

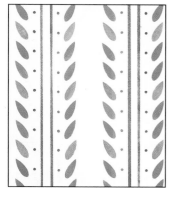

Simple motifs *You can take the simplest of motifs, like the leaf on these two pages, and use it in a variety of ways to give very different effects. Here, it gives a crisp, American country look, thanks to the use of strong colors and a regular, but simple pattern.*

Using color *A more subtle effect is created with color washes: the main wall has a gentle green wash, and stripes have been masked off (see page 87) to take a gray wash. Each leaf is individually stenciled.*

Informal effects *This is a less formal look – the stencil has been scattered within the stripes. Use blending shades of the same color – here they are contrasting shades of soft cobalt and bright ultramarine blue.*

Adding movement (RIGHT) *Although stencils can produce a formal, regular look, they can be used just as effectively to create a design with a liberating sense of movement. If you want a relaxed country look, then this cascade of autumn leaves is one solution. The base color for the wall opposite is a deep red, though the subsequent layers of lighter tinted glazes knock back the color to a subtle, rich tone. The same stencil is used with varying shades of reds and oranges; both color and positioning are deliberately random to produce the impressionistic softness of a freehand leaf storm.*

Beautiful ready-made architectural or naturalistic designs of varying complexity are easy to come by, together with ideas for using them. But designing your own stencils is easy and a source of real pleasure and you can tailor your design precisely to fit its use. It is probably a good idea to start with something small, until you become more confident.

You could commemorate important family events in a purely personal and gratifying way – perhaps a laurel wreath punctuated by rosettes, signed and dated, to recall a prize won at a local show, or a frieze in the kitchen of cherries, strawberries and redcurrants to recall a particularly bumper year in the garden. Or shells and crabs and fernlike seaweed in dusty pink, brickdust red and olive green stenciled round the bath panels could remind you of holidays when the sun shone and the sea was benign.

Planning a stenciled design

In order to work on a large surface, such as a wall, stencils have to be in scale and carefully worked out. Tiny flowers will disappear in a freckled miasma, whereas bold sheaves of peonies held together visually by a heavy stenciled rope border will command respect. A carefully planned and organized all-over pattern looks better than little discrete motifs dotted about. And on a wall, a border or frieze will finish off a design and pull it together.

In the early days, wall stencils were often combined with a regular pattern of stripes or broken lines to emulate wallpaper, or were framed by painted panels and combined with freehand painting. As methods of organizing stencils, these are dramatically successful and confer dignity to the humblest repeat of leaf and tendril. It is all a matter of presentation – as with much decoration, the frame makes the picture. It is a good idea to try out designs on a sheet of lining paper before committing them to the wall or floor.

Skillful cornering (BELOW) *Stencils often look best on a broken paint finish, particularly if they are not completely symmetrical, like this heraldic motif. The walls and ceiling here have a yellow oil glaze that has been rag-rolled: a gentle background for the subtle, stormy colors of the stencils, which come from mixing together purple, blue and brown.*

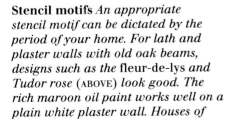

Stencil motifs *An appropriate stencil motif can be dictated by the period of your home. For lath and plaster walls with old oak beams, designs such as the* fleur-de-lys *and Tudor rose (*ABOVE*) look good. The rich maroon oil paint works well on a plain white plaster wall. Houses of later periods – with smoother and larger expanses of wall – can take a concoction of different paints and a mixture of motifs (*TOP*). These were drawn from traditional pattern books; the design is tightly organized with vertical stripes and common denominators of gray and earth tones.*

Stencils can be applied to most painted surfaces. They look particularly good on a slightly broken surface, such as a colorwashed or sponged wall. The paint for the stencils needs to be quick-drying and not too liquid – artists' acrylics are most suitable, or you can use signwriters' colors or car spray paint.

Applying stencils

If you are using different versions of the same stencil for each color, make registration marks through the stencils to be centered over pencil dots on the wall. If your stencils are made from transparent acetate, you may be able to register the positions for the different colors by eye. Hold the stencil flat in place with strips of masking tape at the corners.

To apply the color, use either a stencil brush or a sponge. Take a little color on your brush or sponge, test it on waste paper to make sure that it is not overloaded, and then dab it on to the surface through your stencil until the color is strong enough, though still textured, and all the details have registered. Leave it to dry briefly and reposition the stencil to repeat the process further along the wall. You can speed up the process of stenciling many repeats by cutting a batch of stencils at once, positioning them carefully and doing them sequentially, so that the first is dry by the time you finished the last, and you can return to do a second color.

Finally, protect the finished article with clear matte varnish, or use spray varnish over car spray paint.

SPRAY STENCILING

THIS TINY WINDOW (BELOW) achieves a brilliant combination of maximum light – due to the translucency of the car spray paint – and privacy. The subtle greens that are used for the fern pattern are made up from eight different shades of paint. The lacy border holds the whole design together.

The interior window, right, has been decorated with a ready-made stencil pattern. It is also created with car spray paint, to give it a delicately stippled effect. The success lies in careful masking and parsimony with paint.

A new leaf (RIGHT) *This subtle design uses the simplest of templates – fallen leaves collected on an autumn walk. Sheaves of leaves were stuck temporarily to the wall and painted over with a yellow glaze. For the window surround, a very dry mixture of green, white and a touch of red eggshell paint was rubbed outwards from leaf templates that were cut from paper.*

There are numerous stencils that can be bought ready-cut, but much of the fun of decorative finishes is creating your own designs.

Making your own stencils

To make your own stencils, you will need oiled stencil board or heavy acetate film, a sharp modeling knife or scalpel, a felt-tip pen to draw your design on to stencil board, or an Indian ink pen or Chinagraph pencil for acetate, and a sheet of hardboard or heavy glass (beware sharp edges) upon which to cut. Transfer your design with carbon paper, if you are using card. Acetate has the advantage of being transparent, so you can simply trace it and cut it out carefully with the knife. Multi-colored designs that need a separate sheet for each color are easiest to do with clear film.

Blocking

Another method of repeating a design on a large expanse, such as a length of curtain fabric or the walls of a room, is to print with a block. You need to cut your pattern on something flexible and resilient – for a small design, you can use an ordinary pencil rubber, a synthetic sponge, or even a potato. Cut a surface pattern with a modeling knife, dip the block lightly in paint and print on to the prepared surface. Small motifs – of leaves or stars – printed in this way are fine for a border.

For something larger you can manufacture a more ambitious block yourself from a chunky off-cut of wood, on to which you stick string or heavy piping cord, following the outlines of your design and filling it in with concentric lines. Hard blocks will work best on smooth, flat walls that will take a clear image, although you can always touch up minor flaws later with a brush. For walls with a much rougher surface, opt for a softer block made from a sponge.

A thick paint gives the best results with blocking. Try children's PVA paint as an alternative to household paints, or lino-printing ink for surfaces that are non-absorbent. For fabrics, use acrylic or oil paints, or paints that are specifically for fabrics. As always, experiment with different paint and colors.

BLOCKING

Walls need to be well prepared before blocking – they should be as flat and smooth as possible to take a clear image. The block can be made out of a piece of blockboard with a handle screwed on the back (any simple cupboard knob will do). Make the relief pattern on the block with string (as here) or stick on shapes cut from polystyrene or thick cardboard. For walls with a rough surface try using a block cut from a square sponge.

1 *Draw your pattern on a piece of blockboard. Two diagonal lines marked on first will give a center point for the pattern and show where to screw on the handle later. Stick on string with epoxy glue to make the relief pattern.*

2 *Brush eggshell paint over the pattern on the block. Keep a spare bit of paper towel handy to wipe out excess paint from the loaded brush – this prevents blobs of paint from spoiling the block pattern.*

3 *Mark up the wall first with a pencil (you can remove these marks later with an eraser). Press the block firmly on the wall. A slightly broken finish is part of the charm here, avoiding the formality of a very crisp print, but you can touch it up later with a brush.*

Creating the final look (RIGHT) *The effect of the block pattern can be enhanced by a subtle background. The dark green of this simple paisley pattern is offset by a combination of cool greens on the wall. For the main wall a layer of diluted white emulsion has been brushed lightly over a base of green emulsion; the border beneath the dado rail has a further coat of white wash (see page 87 for masking off and painting borders).*

FREEHAND PAINTING

FREEHAND PAINTING NEEDS a modicum of confidence. You can either create your own motifs – trying them out on paper with colored pencils or water-color first – or you can copy designs that look manageable, in colors that will work with the rest of the room.

Begin by shameless plagiarism. Look around you for simple images that you like – a basket of vegetables from an Elizabethan painting, a bold and primitive bunch of flowers by Picasso – and trace it on to your chosen surface. Traditional painted folkart motifs are also a good starting point for a beginner, because they are usually fairly simple, without pretension and unconcerned with perfection (see page 138). You can enlarge the original with grids and squared paper, or on a photocopying machine.

Museums and antique fairs can be helpful in your search for authentic patterns; if possible, go armed with a camera – a photograph makes an invaluable *aide-memoire* for the exact design, colors and degree of distressing in the original.

Rug hallucination (ABOVE) *This bright kilim is actually a bit of artistic license on a stone floor. The red rectangle was painted first,* *followed by the cream design. Acrylics were used for speed, and the whole design is protected by coats of polyurethane varnish.*

Tudor tendrils (LEFT)
*Local museums are a good
source of original motifs
– this piece of Tudor whimsy
was the result of much
research in the Christ-
church Museum, Ipswich.
The colors were applied
freehand with emulsion
paint, on a plastered wall.*

Creative possibilities
(RIGHT) *Shutters are the perfect place for freehand
artistry – there is something
comfortingly manageable
about those neat rectangles.
This design was penciled
lightly on to the wood first
and then painted in artists'
oil colors. The pink frames
were then applied with a
very dry brush. You can decorate the panels of a door in
a similar way, or perhaps
just pick out the panels
themselves with different
colors. Alternatively, copy
the exuberance of a Florentine door (see page 70).*

Humble medieval churches are often a good source for the kind of thing that will look good in a timber-framed Tudor house. For example, you may find inscriptions or quotations painted in dusty dark gray and pinkish terracotta gouache, in an elaborate frame of painted leaves and scrolls. You can pinch the colors and adapt the frame to border your beams, with perhaps just a pair of gothic initials and the date to signify your proud authorship. Or you may find glorious painted paneling with a saint or two on a patterned ground, surrounded by decorative medallions. Plagiarize the elements you want – the rosettes and diamonds of the background are probably more suitable for domestic interiors rather than the saints – and enclose them within a dark margin punctuated regularly by small gold flowers.

Applying freehand designs

Use masking tape to fix your paper design on to the designated background to see if the colors and proportions look right. If they do, pencil your design on to the background very lightly – pencil marks will not show seriously through the paint. Or transfer the design with jeweler's rouge carbon paper and then copy your design in paint, trying to make your strokes loose and fluent – using a generous-sized good quality artists' paintbrush will help.

For small areas, painting in artists' oils on an oil-based background gives you the greatest range of color, and you can wipe off mistakes.

Free and easy (BELOW) *the joy of freehand painting is that it can be quite casual. These poplar trees have been wiped and smudged for a soft finish; the birds were incised into the paint using the pointed end of a paintbrush handle; and the door frame was completed by roughly applying paint with a dry brush.*

Faking a view (LEFT) *If your house lacks a spectacular view, fake one. This snatch of the country enlivens a long corridor; it was pure invention, but you could copy a photograph.*

***Trompe l'oeil* garlands** (RIGHT) *This deceptive garland adds a touch of humor to a stairwell and leads the eye upwards. The soft colors complement the golden stone.*

CHAPTER THREE

Country Fabrics

COUNTRY FABRICS ARE those that have an affinity with fresh air; that can recover from dogs and children; that give a casual formality to an *al fresco* feast; or that balloon in the breeze from an open window. Very rarely do they stray from the path of natural righteousness – the fabrics that work best in country settings are grown on plants or animals: wool or linen, seagrass or cotton. Usually such fabrics wear well, acquiring character and dignity with the passage of time, and producing soft harmonies of color as they settle into fondly-patched decrepitude.

Natural fabrics look good because they have definite personalities. Upholstery linen becomes bleached and worn by history – the sags and wrinkles of venerable loose covers add to their charm; fine cotton muslin curtains have a particular weight and movement that nothing in polyester can match; sisal and seagrass rasp the feet, but have a stout-hearted reliability that no manmade floorcovering approaches; traditional patchwork stitched on to a woollen blanket hangs and drapes quite differently from any present-day counterpart attached to synthetic batting.

Country fabrics tend to be unbowed by life – linens can be boiled to blinding whiteness, and cottons respond crisply to the traditional touch of starch. Both linens and cottons can usually be unceremoniously washed and line-dried, bringing with them the evocative smell of fresh air – a whiff of pleasure that cannot be applied from a bottle.

Safe and sound (LEFT) *An old English pie safe is the perfect display box for this enviable multiplicity of American patchwork quilts, their colors softened by time.*

PURE FABRICATION

COUNTRY FABRICS HAVE the great advantage of being for the most part affordable. Ticking, muslin and unbleached calico are humble but splendid fabrics, and are so cheap that you can afford to be lavish and to experiment with dyeing, or machine quilting. Cotton velvet takes color beautifully (unfortunately it loses it with less charm) and fine cotton needlecord, with a rich depth of color, is due for a revival. There are expensive country fabrics, too – gloriously floral, up-market chintz, gently-faded Amish patchwork and rich, dark, antique paisley – but a little of each goes a long way.

Often the look that works best in a country setting is evolved from bits and pieces lovingly collected from charity shops and junk stalls. Whereas you may not have time to sit and sew, others have done so in the past, and you might give a good home to a linen tablecloth with a hand-crocheted edge, or a cotton bed-spread resplendent with drawn-thread work.

Searching out natural fabrics

Cultivate an eye for a good fabric – just as a carpenter eyes timber as an adaptable raw material that comes in all sorts of unlikely contexts. Charity shops often have fine old wool blankets – now thrown out by most people in favor of down comforters. In gray or navy they make comforting winter throws for sofas and armchairs, especially if you bind their edges with bright wool and Italianate panache. Look also for genteel floral linen curtains, which can be ripped apart and used for loose upholstery; or lace-trimmed linen hand-towels, which can double as curtains for a glazed door panel. Embroidered sheets, worn by decades of use to a perilous delicacy, can make fresh-looking and washable curtains for a kitchen window. Cotton napkins embellished with satin stitch flowers and French knots may find better use as cushion covers on a bedroom *chaise longue*. But if you should be lucky enough to find old cotton or, better still, fine linen sheets and pillowcases, you can do no better than to use them as they were intended and experience sleep as sweet as it should be.

NATURAL FABRICS

NATURAL FABRICS, in a classic partnership of blues and browns – earth and sky colors – are lightened here by a creamy froth of lace and a bouquet of embroidered anemones. Some of the old-fashioned things have never been improved upon: down-filled, flowered and checkered patchwork quilts; fragrant bolts of crisp cotton, linen and ticking; touchable velvets; briskly-utilitarian coir; and the traditional intricacies of indigo batik.

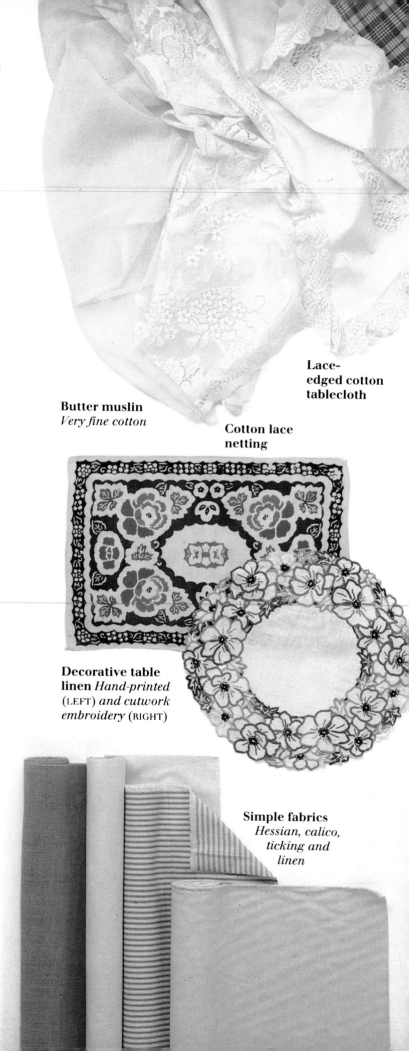

Lace-edged cotton tablecloth

Butter muslin *Very fine cotton*

Cotton lace netting

Decorative table linen *Hand-printed (LEFT) and cutwork embroidery (RIGHT)*

Simple fabrics *Hessian, calico, ticking and linen*

Paisley design quilt (ABOVE)

Cotton eiderdown cover *In indigo check. Made in France in the nineteenth century*

Patchwork quilt *Design relies on alternating large and small squares*

Cotton candlewick bedcover *Early nineteenth-century example with a subtle design of white on white*

Coir matting (RIGHT, ABOVE) *Woven from very hardwearing coconut fiber*

Bedcover *With crewelwork embroidery on linen. Dating from 1710*

Blue and white fabrics *Pure cotton with a design inspired by antique ceramics* (LEFT), *glazed cotton chintz* (CENTER) *and cotton batik – the design is hand-printed by coating with wax areas to be left undyed.*

Turkish rug *In pure wool*

RUGS & MATTING

IT IS A SAD FACT OF LIFE that wall-to-wall carpeting just does not look quite right in a country context. But if the undoubted comfort and convenience of carpets are important to you, there are styles you can choose that will look better than others. Finely patterned or plain wool carpets in country vicarage colors – sage and olive green, faded pink, Wedgwood blue and cream – pull a room together and give it warmth. And cord carpeting comes in a wide range of colors – the dark shades make an excellent foil to jewel-bright oriental rugs.

Terracotta and polished wood have a friendly relationship with humble mats – be they sisal, plaited rush, coir or seagrass – which make the perfect country floorcoverings. You can add color with a mosaic of rugs – garnet and indigo Persian rugs, nicely faded Turkish carpets, or perhaps a collection of kilims.

Making your own rugs

Rugs are friendly to the feet and surprisingly quick to make. They can be made by pushing yarn through the backing fabric to form loops, or knotting yarn on to open mesh canvas, which will form a dense pile rug. Alternatively, simple woven rugs and needlepoint rugs provide a wonderful opportunity to experiment with color. Designs of Vanessa Bell and Duncan Grant in the 1930s are very inspiring, or you can adapt anything from postcards to painted tin trays and enlarge their patterns on to the backing fabric with a felt tip pen. Then copy the original colors with identical shades of tapestry wool. This is an affordable way to emulate the gentle opulence of the Aubusson rugs of France or the brilliance of a priceless prayer mat.

Rag rugs are quick to make and have a solid authenticity – oval rugs made from plaited strips of material in muted colors look good, as do bolder designs with strips hooked or prodded on to a hessian backing. In the old days animal feed sacks were used as backing and the children of the household had the task of cutting piles of worn fabric into little strips that were then pulled through the backing material. (See page 178 for making hooked rugs.)

Painted floorcloths are also a possibility, although there is something slightly cold about their finish.

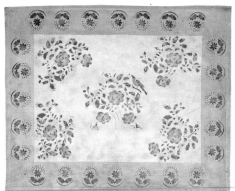

Reviving old arts (LEFT) *Canvas floorcloths were used in America from the early eighteenth century onwards because they were durable and easy to clean. This modern stenciled version has also a light-hearted elegance of color and design.*

Rural charm (LEFT) *Hand-dyeing gives an earthy look to the wool used by Pat Hornafius to make this Pennsylvania hooked rug showing a Holstein cow. The slightly wavering rectangle is characteristic of a hand-made rug.*

1930s' inspiration (RIGHT) *This long, narrow, hooked rug, with its bold diagonals of flowers, was inspired by the colors and designs made by the English artists Vanessa Bell and Duncan Grant in the 1930s, at their country home, Charleston. The bright design is echoed in the sunset-colored walls, which were painted using a feather duster.*

CURTAINS & BLINDS

OUNTRY WINDOWS come in every kind of size and shape, from tiny trapezoid Elizabethan letterbox slits, to generous casements and glazed garden doors. A little thoughtful analysis can help you plan your window treatment. Some rooms are definitely about light and air – summery spaces that need only a fluttery wisp of sprigged muslin at their windows. Other rooms have a stolid and determined character of winter retreat and their windows can take any amount of layered and generously gathered fabric.

Some country windows may look best with no curtains at all. A window that frames a beautiful view can be best served by treating it as just that – a picture frame – with a painted molding. Shutters can have a calming dignity when unsoftened by fabric. Their panels invite freehand experiment with paint.

Window shades
Roller blinds and window shades are simple to make, let in all the sunshine possible, and are very cheap. They look good in rich stained-glass colors and can positively celebrate a strong fabric design. Crisp fabrics are ideal – from ticking and calico to chintz and upholstery cotton. Their strict lines can be softened by a scalloped hem, or – for people who like privacy – by curtains to draw across from the sides.

The horizontal pleats of Roman blinds and the loose folds of Austrian blinds can be made from a wider variety of fabrics. Neither is difficult to make and you can buy kits for the fittings from most furniture fabric stores. Festoon blinds, with their ruched finish, must be approached with caution – they take up a lot of space and light and on a small window can look as if a full-blown galleon is attempting illegal entry.

Full treatment (RIGHT) *Curtains made from humble calico look as rich and generous as these if gathered with theatrical panache. The success of this effect lies in the original dyeing and finishing of the fabric: the curtains were spread out to their full extent on the lawn, and splattered with Wedgwood blue and indigo dye. They were then lined and the tops quilted.*

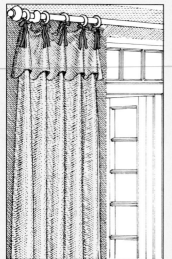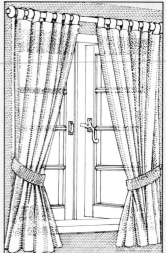

COUNTRY CURTAIN HEADINGS

Blind passion (ABOVE) *The stained glass brilliance of this classic Liberty peacock print is richly intricate by night and glows by daylight. Just to emphasize the effect, there is a rectangle of real stained glass in kaleidoscopic colors.*

Informal gathers *The heading tapes you can purchase may not be the most flattering for your particular curtain. Sheet curtains look best without regular gathers: here the curtain is delicately bunched up by rings, disguised beneath ribbon bows.*

Looping curtains over a pole *For a simple heading, sew loops of the same material as the curtain at the top and thread the pole through. Alternatively, make the loops a feature by using colorful braid, or adding loops to a scalloped top edge.*

Transforming old sheets *Old sheets make summery curtains, especially when – as here – they are decorated by sprigs of embroidery. The sheet is doubled over, and a seam run across the top to make a casing in which to insert the curtain pole.*

Anyone who can sew a seam can make their own curtains. Generally it is best to use a generous quantity of affordable fabric, rather than be parsimonious with something splendid – curtains look best fully gathered and usually hang most interestingly if they can be either bunched on the floor at the hem, or pulled into a good fat curve over a tie-back.

Curtain finishes

Curtains can be decorated in thousands of different ways. Plain cottons can be painted or printed using stencils or potato prints (perhaps repeating designs used elsewhere in the room). Fine fabrics look beautiful embroidered in simple stitches; coarse cotton or linen can be finished with colorful crewel work. Fringes, braid and tassels all give weight and a feeling of luxury, as does the simple expedient of adding a thick lining – a lining will also protect the main curtain fabric from the light.

Unlined curtains

Cotton muslin curtains, either plain or delicately aged in coffee or tea, look light and fresh, but still have enough body to conceal the blackness of night. Their airy pallor has the additional charm of movement – they blow in the slightest breeze in a romantic and sensuous way and look best when they are generously gathered. For more formality, they can be edged with binding. Fine, slightly uneven Indian cotton has a beautiful freshness, and if you can find it in blue and white stripes, your windows will have the cheering brightness of blue skies and seaside sunshine.

Fine embroidered cotton sheets, past their youthful robustness, will make very crisp and summery curtains, if they are boiled to snowy whiteness, starched very slightly, and then, with the decorative edge folded over at the top to show it off, gathered and hung by curtain rings from a pole. Unlined, crisply bordered patchwork curtains glow brilliantly when the sun shines through them, and the delicate tracery of *toile de jouy*, with its scenic pattern on cotton or linen, is a perfect summer material.

Simple, unsophisticated fabrics look most comfortable when they are unpretentiously gathered and hung from a wooden or bamboo pole on hooks through the narrowest and most inconspicuous of curtain tapes. Better still, you can use narrow ribbon threaded through slots in a double-stitched hem and attached to the pole with old-fashioned rings.

Heavy curtains

Winter curtains can be thickly quilted to keep out the cold. Heavy fabrics must reach the ground to exploit their draft-proofing quality and to give life to their stiffness – otherwise they just hang in dull parallel folds. Finishing off hems with wide borders will add weight and depth. Paisley in rich, warm reds and browns takes some of the sting out of winter windows, and if you are feeling clannish, tartans have a surprisingly festive and cheering air.

VALANCES

VALANCES ARE USUALLY shaped like three-sided window-boxes, made out of timber, and attached to walls, window frame or ceiling by angle brackets to conceal unattractive expanses of curtain track. They do not have to be rock-solid – humble hardboard should be strong enough. Then use glue, pins, Velcro and tacking stitches to fix fabric that matches or contrasts with the curtains. If you are very lucky, you may be able to find a handsomely carved length of timber which can be gilded to make a baroque valance (see page 169).

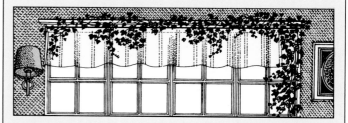

A living valance *The perfect country look – pale muslin is pinned across the top of a window and an ivy trained from a pot on the sill around the whole window frame.*

Fabric valance *Swags of fabric can be used quite casually to create a rich, opulent effect. Fix the fabric with a staple gun and add rosettes or bows.*

Stenciled valance *Traditional motifs taken from American painted furniture transform a wooden valance.*

Pure theater (RIGHT) *This window treatment uses an effective combination of fabrics, hung simply from a bamboo pole. Cheap striped cotton from India was draped over the pole first, and then augmented by an old pink bedspread, generously swagged. The soft, warm colors at the window are partnered by a faded patchwork quilt that covers the 1940s utility armchair, and pieces of antique tapestry which came from a local junk shop.*

QUILTS, PATCHWORK & TAPESTRY

THESE ARE THE ESSENTIAL country fabric accessories: faded tapestry firescreens showing blowzy pink roses; ancient patchwork, the colors softened by time and the mauves completely worn away; and quilts firmly stitched on to their blanket interlining, somewhat puckered with age, or filled with down and weightless, sewn in great swirls on to multicolored cotton like a field of flowers.

The magic of old quilts

Old quilts in pristine condition are hard to come by, but slightly tattered ones still look marvelous and can be admired as wallhangings if they are too fragile to beautify a bed (see page 180 for hanging a quilt). Old cotton quilts tend to be the hardiest – concocted from the clear reds and blue stripes of flannel petticoats and strong collarless shirts. You can always rescue tattered patchwork by repatching it, or – if all else fails – by cutting out any sound pieces and using them to make cushion covers.

Making your own patchwork quilts

There are still patchwork circles – ladies of serious dedication, fanatics one might almost say – who can be commissioned to create your dream quilt. But, in a puritanical sort of way, that is to miss the point entirely. Patchwork quilts can be personal *aides-mémoires* of people, places and times. They are not difficult to make – many of the designs can be adapted to machine stitching – and assembling all those little shapes is an excellent tranquilizer.

Tricolor quilt (RIGHT) *More than a century old, this Cumbrian quilt was made from a traditional combination of patches from red flannel petticoats and blue and white workshirts – the color scheme has a simplicity that looks as fresh today as when it was made. Rag rugs complete a picture of well-worn history.*

Military centerpiece (RIGHT) *This venerable "campaign bed" is a relic of the English officer's life abroad. It can be dismantled and would have been carried from camp to camp. It was bought as a bundle of unidentified pieces of metal and it took all the owner's ingenuity to put it together. Its romantic origins are emphasized by full muslin hangings, dyed in tea; a jewel-bright random patchwork quilt; and beautifully soft white lace and linen pillows. To complete the effect, gothic strands of ivy festoon a beam.*

TRADITIONAL PATCHWORK DESIGNS

MANY OF THE traditional patchwork designs can be sewn on a machine, as long as the shapes are not too small or complex. Choose designs like these, which are based on straight lines, to create a stunning piece of patchwork quickly and very easily.

ROMAN SQUARE

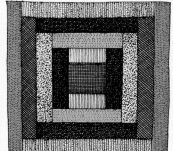

LOG CABIN

PINEAPPLES

If all the patches of your quilt come with a bit of history, the end result will have a benign presence, like a collection of old postcards or love letters. Friendship quilts used to be made by a whole community to celebrate a marriage or a birth, with each participant stitching a fond message into her square to produce an album of memories.

Appliqué and plain quilts

These days appliqué quilts are very quick to make, because some of the stages can be speeded up. Iron-on fabric glues can be used to hold the appliqué in place before sewing it down, and sewing-machine zigzag stitching produces a very respectable finish.

Plain cotton handstitched quilts have a dignified charm, but have to be worked on a quilting frame in order to avoid distortion. The most sophisticated form is the white-on-white quilt – white stitches on white fabric. Colored thread also looks very pretty.

Tapestry masterpieces

Tapestry kits for cushions and rugs are easy to find and come in a huge range of designs. Once you have mastered the very basic skill of the stitches, and have the confidence to tackle the extremely sophisticated art of design and color selection, you can break free of ready-made kits and make your own masterpiece.

Color comes free – and you can be as subtle or as bold as you like, using a mixture of different strands of wool to achieve gradations and softly speckled shades. Probably it is easiest to work from a photograph for the design, possibly with a few changes of your own; otherwise draw your idea on squared paper. In either case, scaling up with grids is a useful way to get the general proportions right. Draw your design on to the canvas with felt-tip pens, allowing a wide margin round the edge of the canvas, and stitch away, starting with the dark colors. The same principles can be applied to tapestry cushions, stool and chair seat covers, or – if you have more time – even tapestry rugs (see page 104).

Recycled seat (RIGHT, TOP) *A Turkish carpet was recycled to make a seat for this unpretentious country rocking chair (see page 178). The colors in the carpet are picked out in the tapestry cushion.*

Country grandeur (RIGHT, BELOW) *The rich and dignified colors of this tapestry throne are the perfect foil for its writhing baroque base. The heavy, formal silk curtains are bordered and frilled in palest aquamarine.*

Stars and stripes (FAR RIGHT) *Simple elements combine to give a summery freshness to this conservatory – the comfortable sofa has a stylish loose cover in humble pillow ticking, and the star-patterned antique cotton patchwork bedspread is casually hung by bulldog clips from a batten.*

EMBROIDERY & CROCHET

THE ARTS OF HANDSEWING are sometimes overlooked in this machine and speed-obsessed age, but they have much to recommend them. The charm of hand-sewing lies in its imperfections – machine embroidery is totally regular and utterly dull in comparison. If you have no time today to undertake elaborate drawn-thread work or tiny stitches in two-ply thread, you can still achieve a worthwhile work of art using tapestry wool and chain stitch, and delicate sprays of tulips and roses can be worked very fast in satin stitch. Cross stitch grows quickly and has a rustic charm, particularly in strong reds and indigo.

Embroidery can be used as a finishing touch – to decorate a hem, or as a practical and attractive edging: blanket stitch could not be simpler and gives a particular finish and fullness to fabric.

Emulate the approach of the French, whose expertise in sophisticated textile crafts is based on thoughtful overall design and scrupulous choice of colors. If the thought of doing your own handsewing is just too daunting, country antique and junk shops often have covetable examples that you can buy.

Crochet creations

Ever since the 1960s crochet has had a bad name, when it became associated with the hippie movement. But fine crocheted lace hangs so beautifully that it deserves a better fate. Crochet lace curtains, used with continental panache, have more of the honest peasant than the hopeless hippie about them. Hunt for patterns for your own crochet work to transform your windows with impressionist sun and shadow.

The easiest, and one of the most comforting crochet creations is the all-embracing Afghan rug. Basically just a square worked from the middle, and firmly edged (with reverse crochet), this is an essential accessory for winter evenings by the fire. Worked in one or two carefully chosen colors, the Afghan has definite designer cachet.

Very keen crocheters can tackle bedspreads, in thick cream or white cotton, and even heavy cotton rugs. These large pieces are usually made up from a number of squares, but they take time to complete.

Drifts of lace

The Victorians were the great exponents of lace with everything. Just as the exteriors of English terraced houses were iced with a delicate filigree of pressed metal on porch and sill, so the interiors suffered from acres of lace. Today you can be more discriminating with lace, exploiting its properties as a visual leavener – a drift of cotton lace curtain softens a window, diffuses the harsh impact of gray days, and blurs the scrutiny of passing strangers. And when the sun does shine, it casts its own dappled net through the weave.

LACE EMBELLISHMENTS

COARSE LACE MAKES a crisp and weighty edging to blinds. It forms the perfect counterbalance to dark, carved wooden headboards or severe, paneled walls. Ushant cottage dwellers in France use an unpretentious band of lace to edge the mantelpiece in their brightly painted matchboard interiors. The Dutch maximize both light and privacy by using lace half curtains, hung from a brass rod. Lace-trimmed tablecloths always bring an air of old-fashioned luxury to candlelit dinners, or carefully presented teas.

The best lace is handmade and adorns pillowcases, bedlinen and bolster covers. Because lace is so time-consuming to produce, there is also a legion of tiny pieces – runners, coasters, nightdress cases, Duchess sets, table mats, and so on. Best avoided as they create a spotty effect wherever they are used.

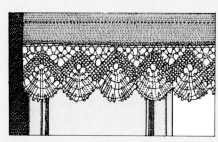

Lace on shades *Look for lace made from heavy cotton (usually torchon lace, as here, or crochet lace) that can be sewn to the bottom of a shade.*

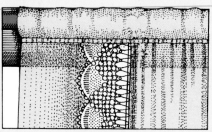

Adding a curtain edging *Use cotton lace for curtains, too: slipstitch it down at the side of a curtain for a delicate, summery finish.*

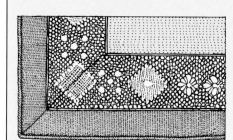

Insertion lace *A ribbon of lace adds a decorative border to a center panel in a cushion.*

Crewel deception (RIGHT) *This half-tester bed is covered, backed and hung with Indian needlework reminiscent of Jacobean crewel work. The backing fabric is thick, creamy wool, which hangs beautifully, and the woolen embroidery colors have a rich intensity.*

LOOSE COVERS, CUSHIONS & BOLSTERS

THE COMFORTABLY SAGGING and nestlike armchair, dressed in a loose cover – faded floral piped cotton, somewhat worn at the arms and wrinkled about the seat – is a quintessential piece of country furniture. So, too, are ancient sofas clad in heavy linen and beaten by years of hard use into dignified submission, shedding the merest curlicue of horsehair from their mysterious frames. Loose covers are best made from any of the traditional, strong cottons or linens. They are time-consuming to make, but should last for years, so it is worth investing in durable fabric and making absolutely sure that you can clean or wash it without shrinkage.

Making loose covers

Loose covers for sofas and armchairs usually look best made in the traditional way, with self- or contrast-piped seams, and tailored or box-pleated skirts to give weight and hide the sagging springs. Prints and plain colors should come from the same color range, and patterns look best if they have the same density of design – but the look to aim for is the friendly harmony of the herbaceous border, rather than the exact particularity of an interior designer's color swatch.

Cushions are the comforting accessories that finish off a room and act as a sort of punctuation mark – to echo a pattern or bring emphasis to a color used elsewhere in a room. Arrange them to lean against languidly in bed, and fill in odd corners with a bolster – lace and lawn and embroidery for your bedroom; silk-velvet, gathered and tasseled at the ends, for your sofa or window seat.

Cushions are the place to show off your textile skills, however recently they have been acquired. Anyone can do enough tapestry to make an upmarket cushion, trimmed with silken rope and cornered with tassels. Bargello work, with its horizontal stitches over varying numbers of canvas threads, is stylish and easy to do and kits come in enough designs to inspire the most leaden heart. Cream, knitted Aran or tightly crocheted squares in a traditional, regular design of bobbles and openwork both look good with paisley. Quilted Provençal cotton has a rich and festive look about it and a square of perfectionist patchwork is manageable by anyone. Embroider a kaleidoscope of satin stitch summer flowers; or an elegant bunch of crewelwork grapes in various shades of indigo. And always (unless you suffer from asthma) go for a down filling for your cushions. Nothing else looks as good or feels as comfortable.

Formal setting (LEFT) *This is a sofa for well-behaved families. Silky, white fabric is a classic foil for a scattering of vibrant tapestry and tasseled velvet cushions. Ornately framed paintings hang neatly in their allotted panels, but the restrained and dignified atmosphere of the setting is subverted by an extraordinary baroque inlaid table placed to one side.*

A cushion mountain (RIGHT) *A reproduction American pencil-post bed, made in Iowa to an early 1800s design, displays a mountain of cushions. Completing the exuberant effect are festoons of lace, a floral needlepoint rug on the floor, and tapestry cushions and soft woolen shawls on the blanket box.*

CHAPTER FOUR

Classic Country Furniture

URNITURE THAT RESTS most comfortably in a bucolic retreat is the sort that has a slightly battered, yet dignified presence. It comes trailing clouds of history – tables that have been dented by collisions with pots and pans, dressers whose corners have been worn to a smoothly rounded patina and whose toggle handles have etched a grooved arc in the paint, and chairs whose stability relies on clever mending with glue and bracing plates.

In general, a look of strength and simplicity is most appropriate for the country: this means furniture of solid wood, carved, stained or painted. Veneers have to be approached with caution, as do fancy details and fussy catches. Modern, pre-fabricated furniture may be practical in bedrooms and kitchens, but it can never achieve the character of old-fashioned dressers and cupboards whose imperfections are part of their charm. Authentic built-in furniture tends to be as old as the house of which it is part, and clogged with the same multiple layers of paint.

It is important not to be afraid of color: the days of ubiquitous stripped pine are over. No longer do you need to strive for the perfect, even finish, wielding blow-torch and paint stripper. Up-market decorators now spend hours learning techniques with paint that approximate the signs of wear and tear, and you will find many decorative finishes in this book that recreate the beauty of aged looks for your furniture.

Creating a civilized corner (LEFT) *The crisp discipline of this old Southern plantation desk is tempered by a comfortable tartan club chair in which to muse.*

FURNITURE DETAILS

LIKE A SIGNATURE, THE additional bits and pieces on furniture – escutcheons, drawer pulls, castors and catches – tend to betray the character of the whole. The problem arises when an urge for the antique, possibly even authentic, becomes an ill-observed parody of the original. This is an area where pretension and fakery tend to draw attention to themselves in disproportion to their importance.

On the other hand, appropriate details can give character and charm to an unexceptional piece of country carpentry. Even such niceties as a length or two of decorative beading – framing a panel or edging a desktop – can act as leavening to a worthy but dull piece of furniture.

Researching details

This is an area where research is well repaid. Jacobean and Elizabethan furniture did not have the ambiguous advantage of machine-made hinges and latches – their character came from the particularities and foibles of the metal- or wood-worker in question. Mending is often better than replacing, or you could get a contemporary wood or metal worker to make a copy of the original.

Delicate bureaus or secretaries of the eighteenth century require cautious handling: fine drop or ring handles are fitting, although modern replacements can look like flimsy forgeries. Grand pieces of eighteenth- and early nineteenth-century furniture are often distinguished by the discretion of their fastenings. In any case, you will find an air of quality and finesse in antique replacement fittings that may make non-matching period authenticity preferable to shiny new uniformity.

Wooden details

Where you are simulating an indeterminate, vaguely genteel period with modern carpentry – building a window seat, or creating narrow kitchen shelves for plates and small objects, or making a bookcase in a chimney recess – the best thing to do is find an equivalent detail and copy it. Perhaps your window seat could echo the door paneling in your Victorian house with an inspired use of similar moldings. The supports for your bookshelves could hide neatly behind more moldings and the shelves be backed by vertical wooden planks for a rustic feel.

Shelves in general can gain in personality from the use of lengths of decorative beading used to define the edges. The Victorians excelled in the use of lacy railway station fretwork, and the simpler designs are not hard to achieve and endow the same richness.

Cabinet handles *Matte black iron* (ABOVE) *and brass* (BELOW)

Drawer pulls *In brass, designed to suit all styles of desks or cabinets*

Ceramic knobs *Plain white, simple knobs are sympathetic to honest country furniture*

Decorative cabinet fittings *Cut glass knob* (LEFT) *and drop ring handle* (RIGHT)

Cupboard knobs *In beech and brass*

Toggle fastener (LEFT) *A simple alternative to cupboard knobs*

Cabinet escutcheon (RIGHT) *In brass*

Borders *For fast, effective decoration of furnishings, curtains and blinds*

Gimp and piping *These trimmings provide the finishing touch to upholstery*

Molded wooden beading *For decorating furniture: distress and color to suit*

FINISHING DETAILS

THESE UNPRETENTIOUS furniture details are the punctuation marks that make the eye stop and register period, character and authenticity. The wrong drawer pull or door handle draws attention to itself, and replacing inappropriate or broken details with something stylish will have an immediate restorative result.

The details have to be applied with an eye to the integrity of the whole. Brass angle pieces look fine on simple military chests, but are obtrusively functional in any other context. Plain ceramic or wooden drawer handles fit in with pine furniture – they even confer dignity on pine-fronted kitchen units – but would do no favors to an arts and crafts chest of drawers or a Gothic sideboard.

The secret is to cultivate a discriminating eye for successful detail and a visual memory for its context. Avoid satin aluminum and bright plastic at all costs. Sort through the rusty bits and pieces at flea markets and be prepared to spend hours with wire brushes, steel wool, old toothbrushes and cleaner.

Decorative hinges *Snake hinges* (TOP), *"H" hinges* (CENTER) *and strap hinge*

Castors *Traditional designs in brass and wood*

TABLE TALK

THE IDEAL COUNTRY kitchen or dining table is solidly built, with heavy, curvaceous legs, and large enough to accommodate children's stacked home-work at one end, newspapers at the other, and supper for seven in the middle. Traditionally, these hardworking tables were made of oak or elm, the planks supported on trestles.

Circular tables for some reason seem more hospitable than rectangular ones, but they have an infuriating tendency to wobble on their stands – above all, stability is essential for a kitchen table.

Practical worktops

Having acquired the father of all tables, you will need smaller companions to go with it: kitchen work stations of the 1940s utility era have a nostalgic appeal, with solid pine legs, roomy cutlery drawers and white or cream enamel tops edged in blue. Another respectable kitchen inhabitant is the kind of narrow pine sideboard found in French farmhouses. It has a deep shelf beneath – highly practical for storing casseroles but not suitable for sitting at in comfort.

Marble-topped Victorian washstands, with a frieze of art nouveau tiles, are at their handsome best doing duty in a bathroom, but they can also function perfectly in a kitchen – they provide the ideal cool surface on which to make pastry, with a cupboard beneath and a handy towel rail.

Tables for all occasions

Elsewhere, tables need not be so stolidly practical. Wicker tables, old or new, are woven in a variety of traditional local styles and sit happily in conservatories and bathrooms. In a living-room or bedroom, tables can be more artful, and take on the role of a horizontal display case for a collection of prized objects. These are rooms where softness is in keeping – where polished wood is possible, but where thick swags of ancient patchwork, used as an undercover and topped by a less precious cotton tablecloth, present a friendlier face. The table beneath such faded drapery need be no grander than a circle of chipboard on a stable base. In fact, anything at all can hide beneath the correct generosity of fabric – perhaps a two-drawer filing cabinet, or a wooden tea chest.

All sorts of things can become tables – just about any kind of sturdy box, a sewing machine stand with a slab of marble upon it, a carefully balanced slice of tree trunk, or a cherub statue topped with marble, or a beautiful *papier mâché* tray, for which folding legs can be constructed (see page 170).

Bucolic baroque (LEFT)
Curvaceous cabriole legs support an endearing 1930s table, around which clusters a clutter of almost-matching dining chairs. The essentials of everyday life have not *been forgotten – the chairs are comfortable, there is space enough to absorb busy details, and midday sun beckons to a simple feast presented on appropriate 1930s china.*

Solid simplicity (ABOVE)
This is the quintessential kitchen table, bought for an absurdly low sum. Once green baize was tacked to it and it was used for shop displays. Now it is polished and *resplendent on turned legs that were cleverly extended by its present owner to give it extra height.*

COUNTRY SEATS

COUNTRY SEATING IS unpretentious. Nothing beats the traditional, capacious country sofa with a small family of roomy armchairs. At its classic best, such furniture is wood-framed, in an unfussy style, and upholstered – with all the horrendous intestinal broil of canvas, webbing and horsehair – and is well-padded with feather cushions. This is the kind of thing to look for at sales and auctions, rather than furniture manufactured during the grim years of foam-infatuation. Loose covers, of related, not matching fabrics, create the right kind of welcoming impression, along with all the cosy paraphernalia of blankets, paisley throws and banks of cushions.

Chairs to relax in

Comfortable armchairs come in all shapes and sizes. Lounging chairs and *bergères* – long, reclining chairs, often with a cane seat, back and sides – are good to sink into after a hard day. So too are faded tapestry-covered wing chairs, whose enclosing sides confer a delicious sense of privacy. Buttoned club chairs, upholstered in leather polished by use, and "sleepy hollow" upholstered tub chairs are somewhat more formal but have their place in the country look, encouraging a fine combination of relaxation and straight-spined deportment.

But the best relaxation of all, after a seriously demanding day, is given by the rocking chair. Rush-seated ladder backs and flower-painted nineteenth-century Boston rockers are perhaps the epitome of simple country comfort. Upholstered Thonet bentwoods, with rounded frame and curved arms have tranquilizing properties for the most harrassed – their metal-framed equivalents were aptly known as

The perfect outdoor chair (ABOVE) *This Appalachian twig chair has such organic rusticity that it appears to have grown out of the* *weathered and moiréd duckboard all by itself. The curvilinear design is surprisingly comfortable, but tough on bare legs!*

ROCKING CHAIRS

THE EARLIEST ROCKERS were simply chairs – usually unrelaxing ladder-backs – with bends attached to the feet. The early nineteenth-century Boston rocker was the first to allow the revolutionary new notion of comfort to influence the design – it has a curved seat and arm rests. Thereafter, modifications and improvements were made: in the 1860s the Austrian Michael Thonet designed the classic bentwood rocker, whose elegant curves were copied in metal – the "digestive" chair. English chair-makers produced their own versions – cane-seated rockers and the swing rocker that sits on a stable base and takes up much less room than a conventional rocker.

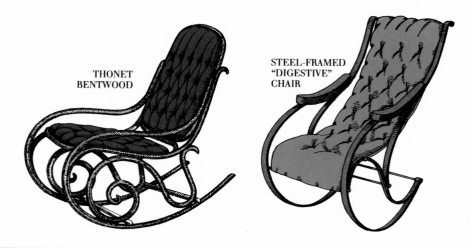

THONET BENTWOOD

STEEL-FRAMED "DIGESTIVE" CHAIR

Sunday afternoon bliss (ABOVE)
*A comfortable corner, such as this –
with a perfect windowseat and soft
chairs – is a must for Sunday after-
noons in the country. The traditional*

*English country chintz was actually a
bargain buy from a warehouse on the
lower East side of New York. The
antique tapestries on the cushions were
rescued from old church kneelers.*

SWING
ROCKER

BOSTON
ROCKER

LADDER-
BACK

AMERICAN CANE-
SEATED ROCKER

"digestive" chairs. Less graceful, but also less space-demanding, are countrified swing rockers, most of which have creaking springs and wobbly bases.

Wicker chairs with squashy cushions make wonderful dining chairs if you have the space. For nostalgic appeal, look for the closely-woven machine-made chairs which were produced after Marshall Lloyd patented his new loom in 1917 in America. These chairs can be given a new lease of life if you paint them in the dusty pinks and gray-greens of 1930s "Art" colors.

Dining chairs

One of the country decorator's first rules is that dining chairs do not have to match. Their essential pre-requisite is comfort – eschew any chair with a seat that is going to cut off your circulation. Windsor chairs, beloved since the eighteenth-century, are hard to beat for comfort and simple elegance. Local variations of style – American as well as English – provide a huge range from which to choose – from simple scroll backs to smoker's bows with bobbined or barley-sugar spindles, all highly polished by years of seat-contact.

Choosing dining furniture

Cane-seated dining chairs can look good and are springy and comfortable, as is rush. Painted and cane-seated Caxton chairs are elegant, with their slightly tapered legs and three simple bars in the back.

Good old benches and pews also suit the country dining room, but do not encourage your guests to linger at the table. Upholstered seating, on the other hand, provides a welcome softness and the chance to use old pieces of tapestry – or even make your own – to give each seat a graceful finish. Thonet bentwoods, their wood bent into elegant shapes, have charmingly patterned or perforated seats which look very pretty, but are guaranteed to give varicose veins.

Smoker's seat (ABOVE) *The rugged masculinity of the elements here – massive brick walls, naked wooden floor and shallow stone steps – makes a perfect back-ground for a nineteenth-century English smoker's bow chair: a low-back Windsor chair that has turned legs and spindles (supporting the arm bow).*

WINDSOR CHAIRS

WINDSOR CHAIRS ARE IDENTIFIED by having legs that are separated from the back and arms by a saddle seat. The earliest Windsors date back to the eighteenth century, soon becoming popular throughout Britain and America. In England they were once the joint result of itinerant "bodgers" (who turned the beech legs), workshop-bound "bottomers" (who carved the elm seats) and "finishers" (usually wheelwrights, who would steam timbers where necessary and construct the chairs). The chairs combine good looks and comfort and were made in a variety of styles, distinguished by the design of their backs. To the basic designs was added a wide repertoire of decoration – bobbin-turned stretchers and spindles, pierced baluster backs, and occasionally cabriole legs. They are chairs for both cottage and castle – the plainest comb-back is as elegant as the most elaborate wheel-back.

SPINDLE-BACK ARMCHAIR

CAPTAIN'S CHAIR

Child's seat (RIGHT) *You might use a special piece of furniture, such as this ornate child's highchair, in a purely decorative way. The highchair's footrest has long gone, though its* anchor holes remain. Its somewhat funereal splendor complements the dark paneled screen in a six-teenth-century cottage (see page 162 for adding paneling to walls).

Commodious seat (ABOVE) *An old-fashioned resolution of elegance and discretion – this graceful cane-seated chair in fact hides a commode. Still to be* found occasionally in antique shops, such seats are a civilized addition to a bathroom and can accommodate most plumbing systems with minor surgery.

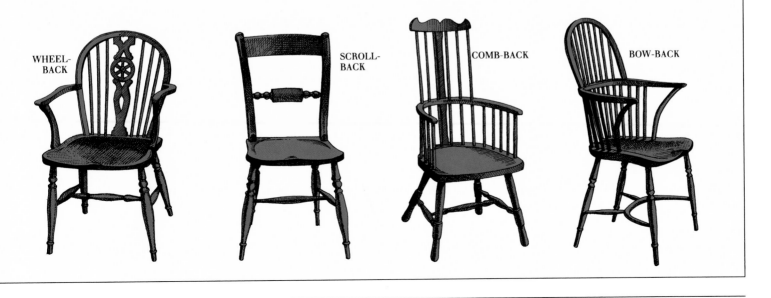

WHEEL-BACK

SCROLL-BACK

COMB-BACK

BOW-BACK

CHESTS, CUPBOARDS & DRESSERS

 A WOODEN CHEST IS THE MOST BASIC and adaptable piece of furniture. Place a chest under a window, with a geranium at one end and a worn velvet cushion at the other, and you have the perfect vantage point from which to watch the world go by. And for comely storage, never despise the humble trunk or old leather suitcases. Whatever their guise, chests and boxes should be solid, and have an air of history.

If the wood of your box or chest is old and battered and has a bit of character, you can strip it down to a dignified silvery pallor and wax it. If it is made from hectic new yellow pine, sand down the surface to remove some of the inevitable polyurethane, paint it with solid colors of household emulsion (distressed around the corners and handles) and then seal the whole chest with beeswax.

The versatility of chests

Chests can be as humble or as grand as you like; they can be immaculately padded and clad in tapestry, festooned with a fringe, and call themselves ottomans (see page 177); or they can be elaborate examples of chinoiserie, in fragrant and moth-deterring camphor wood carved with Chinese medallions and dragons. Solid English oak coffers come carved with a frenzy of

Jacobean-style storage
(ABOVE) *The dark wood and bold carving of this sideboard hark back to Jacobean antecedents. The* *heaviness of the piece is skillfully counteracted by optimistic, sunshine-yellow walls and a glittering cache of Venetian glass.*

Tudor-style storage
(RIGHT) *Antique carved coffers, polished to an impressive shine, find an authentic home in a Tudor* *cottage, where they would very likely have been the only form of storage, other than open shelves and hooks on the walls.*

heraldic motifs and stained black. Some blanket boxes have drawers below, like mule chests, or legs and backs, resembling Swedish settles.

Cupboard love
Solid wood and simple lines and fittings are the hallmarks of the country cupboard. Modern built-in units usually look out of place, though it is possible to make a successful wall-full of bedroom cupboards, for example, using skillfully matched old pine doors, and respectable kitchen cabinets using old cupboard bases and drawers. These may well suit your kitchen better than brand new pine cupboards.

Antique French or painted Italian *armoires*, or clothes cupboards, make the most sympathetic of bedroom furniture if you can find them, and if you have the energy to transport them. Failing perfection,

the Victorians had a genius for mammoth mahogany wing cupboards, fitted with a fascinating interior life of drawers, shelves and compartments, which must bring order to the most muddled wardrobe. For a simpler look, the solution a century earlier was a clothes press – a cupboard with shelves and trays on runners and drawers beneath.

Functional cupboards for the kitchen
Curious utilitarian cupboards of the past can have a benign presence in contemporary kitchens. There is the bacon cupboard, whose tall, shallow shelves once stored sides of bacon. Or dough bins, New England pine bucket benches and the comely American pie safe with perforated sheet metal panels in the doors for ventilation: they all had very specific functions and are full of rustic charm.

Country simplicity: solid wood (LEFT) *This simple corner shelf of curvaceous pine makes a flattering setting for an antique German salt pig and some venerable books. The wall behind is painted with a thin glaze, applied in a loose basket weave of brushstrokes.*

Country simplicity: wood and tin (RIGHT) *Using punched tin in kitchen cabinet doors is a practical American tradition, allowing air in to keep food cool but keeping flies out. It also makes a decorative finish, especially when the doors are left open and the light shines through like stars. Tin can be used in all sorts of unexpected and creative ways – for example, some American homes have ornate pressed tin panels in the ceiling.*

STUDY FURNITURE

AT ANOTHER EXTREME to the solid, utilitarian furniture in your kitchen is the furniture that will sit with some dignity in a studious retreat. Finely detailed cabinets, decorated in the Chinese style using black or cinnabar lacquer, and intricate japanned *papier mâché* desks, painted with exuberant flowers and inlaid with mother-of-pearl, have an ornate beauty against a background of country simplicity.

Every hardworking household needs a desk or two – perhaps a masculine Victorian roll-top with hundreds of quirky drawers and compartments, or a neat little Davenport, with a case of drawers and a sloping writing top. It can sit inconspicuously in a corner of a room and swallow up bills in a tidy way.

Auctions and antique fairs will present you with a baffling choice of solid old shelves and corner cupboards. Those with fretwork are particularly seductive – it is amazing what impact a simple undulating or pierced edging can have. And since life can become dull if it is too worthy, you should spare a tolerant eye for the exuberant baroquery of the nineteenth-century whatnot or *étagère*. Use its three or four tiers of shelves, with their frivolous curlicues, to display plants and tasteful trinketry.

Building your own shelves

Shelving looks best made from solid wood and supported on wooden or cast-iron brackets, or – in an alcove – on wooden battens (masked by a lip batten tacked to the front edge of the shelf). You might embellish the front edge with beading, or shape it with an old-time molding plane, if you can find one and feel practical. If you run molding across the top and around the sides of shelves in an alcove, it gives the whole unit an air of permanence.

Books on display (ABOVE) *This Gothic bookcase has the air of a miniature twelfth-century cathedral. Its original claret-colored glass is broken in places, revealing a few of the handsomely bound books within.*

Ordered calm (RIGHT) *Well-ordered and appealing work places are a moderate inducement to write letters and pay bills. This nine-teenth-century butternut pine secretary is a neat tribute to the civilized way of life and orderly mind of its owner.*

Well red (LEFT) *These capacious step-back shelves were built not by a carpenter but by an actor with a perfectionist eye and plenty of time. The basic design is simple, quietly dignified by touches of beading and brass, and dramatized by startling cinnabar red paint, which is offset by a flick of fir-green in cushions and book covers.*

DECORATIVE SCREENS

Sᴄʀᴇᴇɴs ᴄᴏᴠᴇʀ ᴀ ᴍᴜʟᴛɪᴛᴜᴅᴇ of sins – even that pile of dirty washing in the bathroom – and they can divide a large room into warm and manageable smaller areas. They are also the ideal subject on which to flex your creative muscles. Make a basic shape (see page 171) or find a solid old screen, then enjoy yourself. Try paint effects, edged with bold borders; practise stenciling here where you can easily repaint mistakes; cover your screen with those beautiful old linen curtains which are the wrong shape for any of your windows; stencil some fabric yourself in large and slightly muzzy paisley and cover your screen to match your upholstery. Or you can cover a screen with paper cutouts, like the one opposite.

Decorating firescreens

A firescreen can be a freestanding work of art, adding visual interest to the unattractive black hole of an empty grate, or it can be tailored to fit your fireplace precisely with effective draft-blocking capacities.

There is a charming historical precedent of screens with intricate freehand-painted designs – a vase of flowers, bordered with fake tiles; or satyrs and cherubs, with a simple geometric border. You can turn your own hand to similar designs, or work on an enlargement of a postcard that you particularly like, roughly transferred on to your board. Other ideas can be taken from Turkish carpet designs, or the subtle monotone delicacy of stenciled ferns – anything that translates to a rectangle and has an even density and tone will look good.

Consider, too, using tapestry for a fireboard – you would not need a very large piece. Go for tones that match as closely as possible their surroundings, and colors that have a lingering suggestion of warmth.

Adding eighteenth-century gentility (ABOVE) *A firescreen can cheer an area that otherwise may be a nesting place for depressed-looking dusty dried flowers or apprehensive potted plants. This hunting scene makes a decorative firescreen to shield a delicate complexion from the fierce blast of the flames. Such niceties were thought essential in Jane Austen's day. As it happens, this screen can also do duty as a card table.*

A basic firescreen is simple to make and decorate: an invitingly small and manageable area in which to exploit your creative talents.

Big screen (ABOVE) *Here is the ideal screen – nineteenth-century Spanish leather, painted in subtle, muted colors. The look could be approximated by using découpage figures, and Venetian red- and gold-brushed ornaments to simulate the embossed border. Alternatively, you could use the colors as a basis for freehand experiment, toned down with layers of glaze.*

MAKING A SCRAPBOOK SCREEN

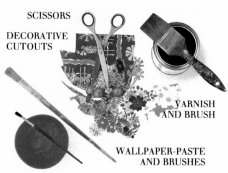

SCISSORS

DECORATIVE CUTOUTS

VARNISH AND BRUSH

WALLPAPER-PASTE AND BRUSHES

Cᴏʟʟᴇᴄᴛ ᴍᴇᴍᴏʀᴀʙɪʟɪᴀ for the ultimate scrapbook screen – photographs, certificates, letters, pictures from magazines, wrapping paper, postcards, menus, tickets and theatre programmes. Sheet music is strongly graphic. Cut out as many images as you need. Plan the background color of the screen so that it sets off the motifs and sand down the surface for an antique look.

Stick on the cutouts with wallpaper paste, composing as you go. For the final finish, apply several layers of satin varnish over the entire screen. Stroke on the varnish, working in one direction and making sure that each layer is dry before putting on the next, so that the final surface is perfectly smooth. You could also add a few three-dimensional finishing touches, like ribbons or rosettes.

The art of *découpage* (ABOVE) *The rich background of this wooden screen was achieved by applying a base coat of white and painting over layers of green, pink and two coats of red egg-shell paint. Then the paint was sanded* *back to let the earlier colors show through an to give the screen an aged look. The motifs are all floral – for a gentle, Victorian look. Several coats of satin varnish protect the screen and give it a rich finish.*

PAINTED FURNITURE

A GREAT DEAL OF THE CHARM of antique furniture lies in the loving care that previous owners have expended on it. Nowhere is this more apparent than in painted furniture – colors and designs carefully chosen, and affection in every curlicue and wobble of the brush. The flowers, the exuberant borders, the bold strokes of Scandinavian *rosemalen* – or "rose painting" – all hark back to the years when there was time for decoration. There was no factory creating millions of identical artifacts – everything possible was made at home out of the materials at hand, and lovingly carved and painted and polished. In those days there was not the feeling that every activity had to be cost-effective, and that approach is precisely the spirit of the country look.

Adding color to furniture

Today, we need to overcome the puritanical insistence on naked wood. Stripped pine is practical for a working kitchen table, but there is no reason why the legs and edges of the table should not be painted.

Stencil kits abound and are a time-honored way of treating furniture – particularly effective in subtle, dark, limited colors. Slightly more complex to achieve are the effects of wood glowing through the negative template that is made by ferns or finely cut leaves:

Simple treatment (ABOVE)
This nineteenth-century New England rabbit ear chair has whimsical ebony edges and bamboo touches to complement its graceful shape.

Subtle stencils (ABOVE)
The solidity of this early American plankseat chair calls for a formal treatment: stenciled decoration in a somber harmony of color.

FREEHAND MOTIFS

MOTIFS FOR FREEHAND PAINTING can be as simple as you like – perhaps a basic border design or naive animal shapes. Often, our forebears tended to soften the outlines of their drawn subjects with dots or tiny curlicues – all adding textural enrichment.

SIMPLE ABSTRACT MOTIFS

AH

MOTIFS TO FIT IN A PANEL

BORDER MOTIFS

Old and new (ABOVE) *This genuine nineteenth-century pine cupboard has been painted in an endearingly fake nineteenth-century manner. It has strong colors, a whimsical distressed finish to the paint, an uncharacteristically asymmetrical motif and a casually marbled top. Although authenticity is splendid, it is not obligatory – a spirited forgery like this can have as much charm as the original, with the advantage of being both affordable and enjoyable to create.*

spray or paint over the foliage – when done well, with a painstaking choice of raw material, this produces a finish with all the filigree charm of handmade lace.

Freehand painting

But the lure to paint furniture lies in the fact that, unlike walls where you have to be able to repeat endlessly the same design to get an even finish, here you may only need to produce one motif whose irregularity is part of its charm – freehand painting is a possibility not to be dismissed. Any book on folk art will show you that perfection is not the aim.

Look for motifs that you like and plagiarize them shamelessly – originality never was part of this tradition. And beyond the familiar motifs of roses and fruit, there are less obvious designs of equal charm – take a quirky menagerie of animals and birds, or the elegant seriffed letters and numerals of Fraktur style, adapted in Pennsylvania in the nineteenth-century from old European illuminated manuscripts. Adding names and dates to your design give it the authentic touch of customized furniture – which is what you are

tackling; you could look for inspiration for lettering on a handsome old gravestone.

Your design should exploit the particularities of the piece of furniture – panels can be painted in a contrasting color and their edges framed by a detailed border; locks and handles can provide a focus for a small flurry of intricate geometry. And then, if you have the courage, worry the finished article with sandpaper to simulate years of affectionate use.

Using colors authentically

There is a perilous line between the vulgarity of folksy and the dignity of folk. A useful discipline is to banish barge-painting completely from your mind and look instead for the mellowed blues and greens of antique Scandinavian painted furniture, the battered scarlet, black, cream and cerulean of French, and the weathered earth and sea spectrum of American. The background color is important and must provide a careful complement to room and painted artifact. Dark colors provide a flattering foil to touches of brightness in a design.

PAINTING A TABLE TOP

EGGSHELL PAINT *thinned with turpentine*

PAINT BRUSHES

DUSTING BRUSH

SANDPAPER AND BLOCK

MATTE VARNISH AND BRUSH

THINK OF A TABLE TOP as a blank canvas for your own designs. Most surfaces can happily take a paint finish as long as they are not too waxed. Remove any wax with turpentine and steel wool, then clean with a rag; always work in the direction of the grain. Remember to use hardwearing paint for tables which will be in constant use – eggshell paint or powder paint mixed with varnish.

1 *Mark up your design in pencil on the table, drawing on guidelines if the pattern has to be centered. Thin the eggshell paint with turpentine for subtle color shades and apply with a fine brush. Leave the paint to dry thoroughly.*

2 *Sand back the paint, using either sandpaper or a sanding block. Go with the grain and apply very light pressure – remember there is just one layer of paint – until you have the right amount of subtle color left in the grain of the wood. Then dust the surface of the table to leave it scrupulously clean for the next stage.*

A taste of Scandinavia (RIGHT)
This basic oak table has been given a new identity – reminiscent of painted Scandinavian furniture – by using subtle colors and a simple design. Oak is especially receptive to this kind of paint finish, because of its deep grain which holds the color after the surface has been sanded back. Humble pine furniture can also work well: originally country furniture was painted in order to hide the poor quality of the wood, rather than for decoration alone.

3 *Cover the entire surface with a coat of matte varnish. This will protect the surface – particularly important for tables in constant use – and also give the table a mellow, "antique" finish.*

CHAPTER FIVE

Collections and Display

COLLECTIONS HAVE A WAY of creeping up on a person. For example, pieces of cheap and decorative Chinese stenciled enamel might be proliferating in odd corners of your home without you really noticing: in a moment of inspiration you put them together, and make the ancient and satisfying discovery that the total is greater than the sum of the parts.

These days collections have become big business and canny antique dealers are wise to every turn that the country collector's fancy may take. It is a real test of ingenuity to find something to collect that has not already been prettified and polished by some antique dealer and given an extremely creative price tag.

This is part of the real pleasure of collecting – looking for beauty where no one has noticed it before. It is the pleasure of the hunt, getting there before the dealers, finding unlikely sources, cultivating junk shops and jumble sales, and discovering job lots at auction – garage and flea market sales often yield unsuspected bounty. You must learn the devious art of the casual inquiry – asking about a handful of objects among which the object of your quest lurks inconspicuously.

The best collections are those that have gradually come about, where each item has a sentimental pedigree, perhaps associated in your mind with a sunny afternoon when you and a close friend just happened to be passing a junk shop. The objects thus acquired become keys that unlock affectionate memories.

Light effects (LEFT) *Sunlight from the window adds sparkle to these antique lamps and dramatizes the strong silhouettes of the reproduction weathervanes (another example is below).*

SHOWING OFF COLLECTIONS

AT BEST, COLLECTIONS are the decorating equivalent of jewelry, and are constantly added to and lovingly shown off, shining with devoted care. Bear in mind that with collections of practically anything, display is almost everything. Your exquisite nineteenth-century samplers will look like tattered old rags unless they are proudly shown off in complementary frames (see page 148 for decorating frames).

One collection may become the catalyst for another. A crowd of tiny thematic objects – for example, the multitude of little antique pigs that started off as a peevish joke – will drive you mad unless they are arranged well away from dust, expansive gestures and exploring childish fingers. Now you need to go back to the auction rooms and junk shops to find idiosyncratic old shop fittings, glass-fronted and brass-handled, in which to display your treasures.

Making the most of collections

First of all, you need to take a long look at what you have and grasp its essential character and particularity. For example, glass and sunlight together make a glittering prismatic show; by comparison, unlit glass

Displays above windows (BELOW) *All sorts of spare surfaces and ledges make effective display areas for collections. This window frame provides a perfect setting for a charming frieze of tiny wooden houses – a miniature example of ribbon development.*

Cupboard display (LEFT) *There is a solemn humor about American folk artifacts that makes a happy partnership with a simple pine step-back cupboard. The combination of straightforward design and sophisticated color produces a look which is, in the best Amish tradition, plain but strong.*

Displays on stairways (ABOVE) *A staircase can be the perfect place to indulge in rococo excess. Here, full use is made of the wall space and ledges. A stained glass panel casts an ecclesiastical light on a motley collection of tracts and artifacts.*

Light show (RIGHT) *This rare collection of antique candle molds, rush light holders and candlesticks includes courting candlesticks, which can be pre-set to burn a certain length of time. Massed candle-power is notoriously seductive: look for affordable reproductions.*

has no sparkle. So a collection, say, of cut glass jars and containers might be shown off to advantage on glass shelves across a window, or where the sun traces an early morning arc. The brightness and glitter of lit glass is doubled when backed by mirrors.

Colored glass, like sapphire Bristol glass, glows brilliantly against the light. Consider achieving a similar effect by filling clear containers with brightly-colored antique marbles or, in a bathroom, with a rainbow of bath oils.

Wall displays

Faded patchwork quilts and fragile kilims look splendid against a wall that softly echoes one of their colors – they need to be hung with care. Battens hung by chains from the picture rail, or screwed into the wall, and then stapled with Velcro are one answer; the fabric can then be carefully sewn to the corresponding strip of Velcro (see also page 180).

Pictures and their frames need to be assembled and displayed with a sensitive eye. There should be a common denominator or two for a collection – period, color, mood or texture – and the frames should echo the paintings in some way (see the example on page 148). Think also about a toning background color to bind the whole composition together.

A single, favorite painting can be a good guide to the color scheme for a room – after all, color is the painter's profession. It is worth analysing the range and proportions of colors used, so you can emulate them on wall and windows, in paint and fabric.

Unexpected treasure troves

The humblest of objects can assume new qualities in a sympathetic setting. Old painted sweet tins and tea or biscuit caddies come in a glorious range of rich color and intricate pattern, which – when jumbled together – can look like nothing more splendid than a

Old frame (ABOVE) *The charm of this modern version of an American theorem painting – stenciled flowers on velvet, in subtle colors and naive shapes – is perfectly partnered by an unusual antique frame with a battered metallic finish.*

A triumph of wallpower (RIGHT *and* OPPOSITE) *Two corners of the same room: the warm terracotta walls, dry-brushed with diluted magnolia emulsion, make a textured background for an excess of art. The wall color echoes details in many of the paintings, while the tapestries reflect the living plants; there is also a friendly harmony in the elderly gilding of the picture frames. Not an effect to be achieved instantly, but one that expresses a fascination for color on the part of the owner.*

Custom-built frame
(ABOVE) *New frames, based on antique precedent, are easy to paint, given practice and a bit of energy. The dark and dignified frame around this Pennsylvanian Scherenschnitt cut-paper picture by Blanche Turner, celebrating a wedding, has been simply but effectively painted using two colors.*

garage mechanic's tool repertoire. A moment's deliberation may reveal that the whole lot will fall into an ordered spectrum of colors, with a preponderance of chestnut brown. A lighter shade of that warm brown dry-brushed (see page 78) on the wall will make a perfect background for the tins, and will warm up the rest of the room.

Keys are another classic example. Most people have a motley collection of unidentifiable keys, some of which – particularly the blackened and notched iron ones – have a certain charm. You may find that yours look handsome hanging from regular rows of nails hammered into a white-painted wall.

Or shells. Few people can resist leaving bracing seaside holidays with a sack full of assorted molluscry. In wind-powered seafaring days shells were used as ballast, and grand landowners would have a dankly mournful grotto or quaint rustic hermit's cell constructed, in which to display their international booty. There are humbler ways to display your collection: a fan of shells can look very pretty laid out on a windowsill or you might cram them in a glass jar and place it where the sun can reveal their translucency.

Enhancing a picture
(RIGHT) *The frame, decorated in the sequence below, gives a classical look to this hand-tinted 1930s photograph. The paint and paper technique will enhance inexpensive prints, an illustration from an old book, or perhaps a piece of tapestry. Choose a clear image that will not be overpowered by the decoration on the frame.*

DECORATING A PICTURE FRAME

Simple picture frames can be transformed by a variety of finishes to enhance the particular mood of a picture. Some techniques will look better on a flat frame – for example, paint effects like sponging or combing. Here, the frame is made from wooden molding (see page 180 for making frames), for a more solid backing. The edge of the molding was first painted gold; then a strip of wallpaper was stuck on the frame. Choose from the wide range of wallpaper designs for an effect that is not as difficult or expensive as traditional gilding, but just as convincing. Subtle additions of paint and varnish combine to give the illusion of an antique, hand-painted finish.

1 *Cut a strip of wallpaper to fit the width of the molding and stick it to the frame with wallpaper paste (just add water to ready-pasted wallpaper).*

2 *Use oil-based paints, thinned with turpentine, to paint over the wallpaper design in related colors – this will give it a hand-painted look.*

3 *Cover the wallpaper with a sepia-colored varnish (made with satin varnish mixed with a small amount of burnt umber oil paint) to give the frame an antique finish.*

SHELF DISPLAYS

 SHELVING CAN BE a simple way of giving a flattering common denominator to a collection of objects, especially if you cover the shelves with fabric, paper, felt or baize. You can achieve a splendid effect quite casually by stapling fabric to the shelves, but you do have to take care (with the corners and the top and underside) and aim for professional perfection, otherwise they can just look tacky. Once upon a time people would line the edges of their built-in bookshelves with fillets of carved wood or strips of embossed leather. You could do the same, or use a wallpaper border or braid. Again, it has to be a perfect job. Measure the edges you want to decorate carefully and miter any corners cleanly. Choose brass tacks to attach leather and braid, and glue for paper borders.

Old china begs to be displayed on a venerable Welsh dresser; it is a good idea to be disciplined about the range – blue and white always quickens the pulse, but there are more esoteric alternatives. The exuberant work of English 1930s lady potters (Clarice Cliffe, Charlotte Rhead, Suzie Cooper) or the clean line and colors of Fiesta Ware from the USA, are bright and exhilarating and look wonderful against a wall dragged, or painted very solid and matte in a toning color. In the 1930s *eau de nil* was a favorite color, as was a particular warm cerise.

Transforming plain china

At the other extreme, a black background and shelves make the color of their contents sing out – particularly if the china comes in warm autumn colors. If the china is predominately white, displaying it against a white background will make it look curiously grubby and inconsequential. But the most everyday white china can be piled on green baize-covered shelves and will gain sparkle and glamor from the contrast.

Shelves that flatter (RIGHT) *Simple shelving and cupboards, home-built in pine boards, are a classic country device. These are stained with a slightly translucent white oil-based glaze that shows up the knots and the crisp severity of black hinges and latches, while flattering the fine detail and quiet colors of their contents.*

Shelf awareness (LEFT) *The wall behind these shelves was once flesh-colored, as a result of which all the objects melted into their background. After the wall was repainted with a carefully chosen green, the ceramics and glassware sprang to shining life. The paint is thinned acrylic, slapped on with a big brush and then wiped off roughly with a rag.*

HOUSEHOLD COLLECTIONS

OLD-FASHIONED KITCHEN tools and receptacles are always satisfying to collect and the less pretentious the display, the better it looks. Butcher's shop fittings provide the perfect combination of storage and display, and will absorb a clutter of jugs and colanders, festoons of dried rosemary and thyme, as well as hefty and dignified black enamel pans and willow baskets, and look all the better for it.

Kitchen ephemera

Kitchens are tempting sites for displays of ephemera – collages of bright labels or orange wrappers, filched menus, or stacks of decorative tins. A huge felt-covered pinboard – either criss-crossed with elastic held in place with drawing pins or stuck with baize or fabric and studded with thumb tacks – could bear an anarchic collection of tickets, theater programs and postcards, or a careful composition of exotic sunset or food postcards. Discarded printers' type cases can make a grateful setting for really tiny treasures: you can hang them vertically, or use them as drawers on wide shelves.

But the problem with kitchens is that everything can get very dusty and sticky. Cleaning a myriad of little objects on open shelves can sour the sweetest temper. The alternative, if you want to admire a dust-free hoard of, say, egg-cups with amusing chicken motifs, is glass-fronted shelves and cupboards.

Collections in bathrooms

Bathrooms are the perfect homes for collections of precious tiles, for example the bold, art nouveau designs of William de Morgan. Victorian tiles in a limited color range make the richest patchwork; a tapestry of tiles in warm browns and reds, or deep green and indigo, is a glorious and practical way of finishing a side-table top, or of making a surrounding for your bath tub and wash basin.

Bathrooms invite frivolous and amusing collections: of ducks and swans, shells and fish. Or you may feel that baskets of fragrant pearly soap may be more appropriate. Think also about making exuberant displays of bathroom packaging – decorated soap boxes, glass-stoppered bottles, or an alchemist's array of prettily labeled pots and jars. They cost the manufacturers big money to produce and design, and they are just about the prettiest visual treat you can lay hands on for nothing.

Bathtowels and bedlinen have a comforting charm about them – shelves full of neatly folded, color-coordinated towels and embroidered sheets and pillow cases, studded with the odd lavender bag, can look beautiful in their own right, particularly if they are ranged in an old armoire whose shelves have been covered with fabric.

A Dutch crown (ABOVE) *Once intended for hanging decomposing game, this gruesomely named "Dutch crown" is now put to less malodorous use displaying a spectacular array of antique kitchen equipment. Cooking paraphernalia does not have to be ancient to be beautiful. A carefully edited collection of modern enamelware can look just as good and does not need to be polished. Add bunches of herbs or strings of garlic and onions for a suitably rustic look.*

Well-dressed (ABOVE) *This vast dresser had to be cut to size to fit into position under the low beams of this ancient kitchen. The walls and dresser were painted a parsley green that gives freshness to an impressive collection of white jelly molds. The green also complements the earthenware and a handsome cinnabar-red Chinoiserie clock. The jelly molds have other uses too: one makes a bowl for potpourri.*

French cuisine (RIGHT) *Handy for the long-armed, this batterie de cuisine has unexpected charm – a glittering tribute to its owner's originality and the unsung appeal of aluminum. The air of an ancient French kitchen is deceptive: although these beams were culled from elderly collapsing buildings, the house itself is new.*

FLORAL DISPLAYS

PLANTS AND FLOWERS HAVE always been the answer to hiding unattractive corners and ugly plumbing, and are an instant method of softening and prettifying hard lines and gappy arrangements. They are also a way to create a visual punctuation mark – a winter windowsill with snow outside looks fine, but becomes a work of art with a semi-transparent scarlet begonia against the snowlight.

Plants are an area where one should be ruthless – it is too easy to become a halfhearted horticultural charity with windowsills displaying wilted geraniums, all elbows and knees, and a leggy and venerable busy lizzie given to you by the lady next door. Keep only the ones that have survived neglect, and resolve to be kinder to them – geraniums are happy to be mostly ignored, and are absurdly grateful for the odd dose of fertilizer. Similarly, *Streptocarpus* spp. (Cape primroses) have elegantly wayward foliage and insist on flowering under adverse circumstances.

Plants look best in groups – a basket full of African violets makes an impact in a way that no single plant can manage, however nicely potted. If three china-blue hyacinths look and smell wonderful, think what twenty will do in a handsome blue and white footbath. Lily-of-the-valley can be induced to flower indoors – try a great trough of them, interseeded with grass. Tureens full of snowdrops have a delicate perfection: you can examine them closely in a way that only the most foolhardy would do out of doors.

Indoor gardening
Find plants that like the same sort of conditions and plant them all together, or mass them in a large container – aspire to something like an indoor garden. A large *Ficus benjamina* (weeping fig) with an elegant droop to its branches, would look good in a big terracotta pot underplanted with ivy. *Sparmannia Africana* (African hemp, known in America as window linen) is an obliging evergreen plant with big lime-green leaves and the occasional cluster of white flowers in summer. It can grow big enough to screen you from the world outside. *Passiflora caerulea* (passion flower) can also be used as living curtains. Grown on wires across a window, this tendrilled climber will fling itself up to a great height and in sheltered sunshine it will bear masses of its strange, fragrant flowers, and cast a pleasing dappled shadow. Lilies in pots are a glamorous option. The trumpet varieties are happy to be grown thus, and can be brought indoors to fill a room with sweetness.

Homegrowing
Experiment with seeds. There is no rule to dictate where plants must be grown, and there is no thrill to match the magic of germination. If you can find a

Feathery larkspur
In a pastel 1930s vase

***Tradescantia* spp.** (ABOVE, TOP) *Hardy and decorative pot plants that grow fast*

China jugs (ABOVE) *Often hand-painted, in a variety of traditional styles*

Glass vases (LEFT, ABOVE) *Keep the glass sparkling clean by adding a drop of bleach or vinegar to rinsing water*

Fruit arrangement *In a simple, hand-decorated bowl*

Lilac blossoms *White blooms always look fresh, especially in vases with plain, strong colors like this green ceramic fish*

Herbs *Make a decorative and practical display; keep parsley (BELOW) fresh in water*

Calathea makoyana *With a wonderful contrast of dark and light green on its leaves*

Anemones *Add a brilliant glow of undiluted color*

Begonia rex varieties *With dramatic, brooding colors.*

Old gardening tools *Have a charm that nothing in plastic can equal*

Vegetables *Arranged in an antique china basin*

Primulas *Flower between mid-winter and summer and look best in groups*

CHOOSING CONTAINERS

For any kind of still life – a mosaic of vegetables, a Christmassy mountain of russet fruit and nuts, a vanilla-scented posy of daphne and early quince flowers, the full rich cornucopia of a summer border, or an autumn *aide-memoire* in the form of dried hydrangea heads and seed-pods – you need containers.

Keep a vigilant eye open for unusual receptacles: the handsome white ceramic buckets that used to lurk in old-fashioned commodes are perfect containers for large pot-plants; gaudy red and gold olive oil tins can become flattering vases for scarlet peonies and poppies; almost any fruit looks good in a basket of some kind; chemists' paraphernalia of phials and philter bottles have a simplicity that is very kind to single perfect specimens of *Aquilegia* spp., or monkshood or papery scarlet anemones, glowing like stained glass when you put them against a window.

light enough spot in your home you may be able to
grow perfect indoor specimens of your favorite
outdoor plants. Twining plants on wires or trellis
around a window is fun (morning glory is good); you
can even try growing edible plants, like French beans,
across a window.

Herbs are, of course, essential country kitchen pot
plants. A sunny windowsill can provide you with
basil, thyme, chives, salad burnet and French
tarragon, preferably tightly-packed and jostling in a
long terracotta trough.

Beautiful effects with foliage plants

Naturally, flowering plants should be chosen with an
eye to enhancing the existing colors in the room. But
some foliage plants have a distinctly designerish cast
to their leaves – the glaucous gray-greens of *Aechmea*
and *Tradescantia* spp., the finely-netted foliage of
Fittonia verschaffeltii and silver-speckled ivies in
great swathes, all look beautiful with plain white or
pink-washed walls. Boldly-patterned foliage has a
startling affinity for classic paisley prints – try russet
and blue-green species of *Maranta, Calathea* and
Caladium and the somewhat sinister *Begonia rex* in
all its exotic banded and spotted manifestations.

Movable feasts

The ephemeral decorative charms of fruit and
vegetables are often overlooked. There is beauty in a
straightforward arrangement of dark shining fruit and
vine leaves on an oval dish, with the great plus that
you can eat your art and create a new masterpiece
with your next shopping trip. Look at eighteenth-
century Dutch paintings and glowing impressionist
canvases for inspiration. Remember, too, your
unwieldy collection of baskets – they have a natural-
ness that makes the perfect foil to mounds of vivid
vegetables and fruit.

Making the most of fresh flowers

Fresh flowers should ideally be picked by yourself at
dawn or dusk in your garden, using florists' scissors
or pruners. To make the flowers last as long as possible, you should do your picking armed with a bucket
of tepid water, so that the stems do not have a chance
to seal up before you put them in vases. Cut hard
stems diagonally, and bash the cut ends of rose stems.
Violets, hydrangeas and lily-of-the-valley like to be
completely immersed in water, heads and all, at least
for a bit. On returning home, and with any bought
flowers, the first thing to do is to recut the stems
under water, and preferably put the whole bunch
somewhere cool and dark for a few hours. This will
allow the stomata to close up and mean that moisture
loss is kept to a minimum.

Homegrown flowers are always best – they have
character and their wayward individuality makes for
grace in an arrangement. Store-bought flowers are
always stiff and perfect and lacking in charm. The
most thrilling cut flowers are branches of fruit

Wayward glamor (LEFT)
Lilies are the filmstars of the flower world – exotic, startling, and often overpoweringly scented. Their speckled beauty is fascinating at close quarters, though their pollen stains in maddening fashion. They suit a certain formality and ruthlessly upstage any floral companion.

Wild flowers (RIGHT) *Do not despise the decorative potential of wild flowers. There is no need to plunder rare species: pick only from plants you find in abundance (taking care not to harm the plants). Try pink and white campion, poppies (pick in bud and seal their stems with a flame), and foxgloves. Hops, rose hips, autumn maple foliage, holly and yew, all embellish a particular season with color and grace. There are countless frothy white umbellifers – like Queen Anne's lace or the hogweed here (treat with caution) – which add a lacy softness to more predictable flower arrangements.*

Simple pleasure (LEFT)
There is an irresistible charm about a bunch of marguerites unceremoniously jammed into a jug. The whole tribe of daisy flowers, with their childish simplicity of form and innocent faces – asters, delicate cosmos, unwieldy chrysanthemums – share this delightful appeal.

Do-It-Yourself Techniques

UNLESS YOU HAVE TRIED, YOU cannot know the pure pleasure of making things. It answers some primitive need, and a piece of work well done leaves you glowing with virtuous creativity. Echoes of those spartan make-do-and-mend, postwar years have left a lingering memory of the satisfaction conferred by putting two unusable things together, and making a glorious hybrid. Flexing one's ingenuity, tidying up loose ends, charming away ugliness: do-it-yourself can answer all these needs and actually result in a creation of which you can feel proud.

The problem has always been not in the endeavor itself, but in the objectives and methods. The joy of using up all those old floorboards, and that length of linen hoarded from the house before last, may just blind you to the fact that you are creating a hideous monster, nothing like the Biedermeier ottoman you have in mind.

Making plans
You have to be clear about what you want to make, or how you want to change the existing object of your attention – make drawings, try colors, or copy and adapt appealing ideas from books and magazines.

The cut-away diagrams that follow give details for the construction of different ideas. If you are feeling creative, use the ideas as starting points rather than exact examples to be copied – just as these items were inspired by the ingenuity found in the homes illustrated in this book. And the possibilities for extra decorative finishes are endless.

Perfection is not necessary, though it makes good sense to tackle a job whose size and complexity do not depress you. Aim for something for which you feel competent, and which excites you. Visualize the finished object and the improvement it will make to the quality of life. It can also help to make a rough estimate of the time required to complete the work. Most of the ideas that follow are concentrated weekend-sized, and should not require you to move out of the house.

The satisfaction of do-it-yourself
What you make will inevitably have a personality of its own – an attribute that is finally beginning, in this mass-produced culture, to be valued. Hand-made things, created with good taste and panache, have character: look at any interior designer's portfolio, and you will find that a penchant for festoon blinds and matching fabric on furniture, walls and windows – the tired old predictable clichés – are bearable only when enlivened by strong dashes of the owner's character.

Do-it-yourself is, in a literal and satisfying way, what home-making is all about. It means fostering a good relationship with your home, bringing out its good points and disguising its bad. A house that is loved and fussed over and looked at with fresh eyes from time to time, such a house will repay your attention with a generous welcome whenever you step inside the front door. Not a bad conclusion to a day spent exasperated by trying to find missing tools, and covered with paint splotges.

A note on buying softwood
You can buy either planed or sawed (unplaned) softwood. The lumber yard will still refer to the measurements of the sawed version even when selling you planed softwood, because the amount that is planed always varies slightly. The following projects give the sawed measurements, but you should buy planed wood (for its better appearance) and then remember to allow for the difference when you draw up any plans. Use the rough, sawed wood only for jobs where the wood will not be seen. For hardwood, the planed version actually is the size by which it is described.

RESTORATION TECHNIQUES

DADO PANELING

WIDE TONGUE-AND-GROOVE boards give a traditional look to this dado treatment. For best-looking results, re-use old boards. Their shrinkage will be minimal – compared with new boards. The framework is ideally of 2 × 1 in (50 × 25 mm) tanalized battens. Fix the ends of the battens first to support their length and leave you a free hand.

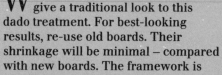

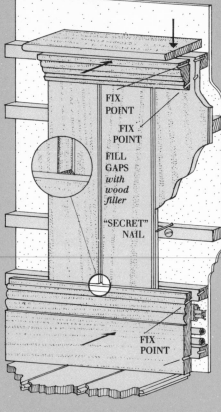

FIX POINT

FIX POINT

FILL GAPS *with wood filler*

"SECRET" NAIL

FIX POINT

2 *Align the first board with the top batten and "secret" nail through the tongue into the battens behind. Push the next board's groove into the first board's tongue, using a hammer to ensure a snug fit. Fix board as before. Fix dado rail molding and skirting board, punching home nails with a nail punch and filling the hole above the nails with wood filler.*

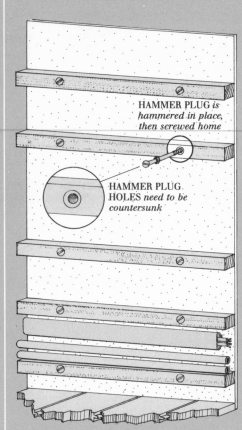

HAMMER PLUG *is hammered in place, then screwed home*

HAMMER PLUG HOLES *need to be countersunk*

1 *Fix battens parallel to each other, using a masonry drill to drill through the battens and wall together. Secure with hammer plugs.*

WALL PANELING

THIS FRAMED PANELING technique is particularly effective on either side of a dividing wall.

Before you add color to the paneling, you may want to distress the wood (see page 50). For an aged look on real oak, use either ammonia or caustic soda (but note that both are extremely hazardous and expert assistance must be sought first). Or imitate woodworm by using a small drill bit – although this may take some explaining when you come to resell your property!

The final finish will be very much a matter of personal taste. Experiment with stains on scraps of wood first, before you attempt any definitive finish on the wall itself. You may find that a decorative bravura finish may look better than a plain wood stain – convincing grain effects are not easy to achieve.

1 *Draw out the design on the wall, dividing it into equal panels – check for accuracy with a spirit level. Plan to attach the top and bottom horizontals of the frame first, making sure that the screw fixings are centered above each proposed vertical frame section. Hide the fixings with dowel, as described in step 2 below.*

Measure the depth of your screw recesses and cut lengths of dowel to ¹/₂ in (1 cm) longer, so they protrude from the holes like traditional pegs.

For a decorative finish, use a plane to chamfer the lower edge of the top horizontal and the top edge of the lower horizontal, then glue and pin flat beading to each horizontal.

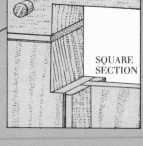

SQUARE
SECTION

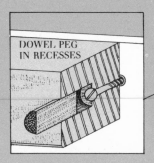

DOWEL PEG
IN RECESSES

2 *To make hidden screw fixings, first drill out ¹/₂ in (1 cm) of wood at the points to be fixed, using a steel dowel bit. Drill standard size holes for the screws you are using, through the center base of these recesses. Place the horizontal section against the wall and punch a nail through the holes to make a mark on the wall at each point. Using a masonry bit, drill the wall, insert plastic wall plugs, then align the wood section and screw home. Inject a little wood glue into the hole and twist in lengths of ¹/₂ in (1 cm) diameter dowel.*

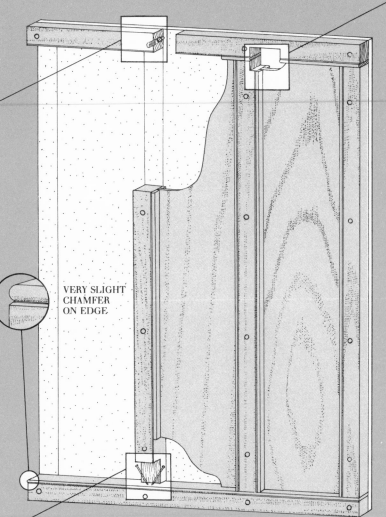

VERY SLIGHT
CHAMFER
ON EDGE

4 *Nail square section along the rear edge of each vertical section. This will maintain a space between each panel and your wall – especially important if the wall is uneven. Place the panels against the square sections and nail on a strip of beading along the sides of the vertical sections to keep the panels in place. This beading will hide the nails added in step 3 and should match the round-edged, flat beading used on the horizontals, to give the paneling a professional-looking finish.*

SKEW NAILING

3 *Measure the length of each vertical frame section separately – they are bound to differ marginally in an old house – and cut to make a firm fit. Mark out the vertical fixing points on each, making sure they are at the same point on each section. The verticals are chamfered and fixed in the same way as the horizontals, except that you should cut and shave the*

dowel plugs flush with the surface. Then nail through the verticals into the horizontals at 45° – the nail heads will be disguised by the decorative beading that is added later.

REPAIRING SIMPLE CORNICES

PLASTER MOLDINGS make a visual punctuation mark between walls and ceiling in the rooms of some period homes. You can repair minor cracks in moldings with plaster filling; to make good larger patches you will need to use a mixture of plaster of Paris and jute scrim – and make a template as shown in this technique.

First saw out the damaged area of the plaster to give a clean edge. Nail a temporary wooden batten to the wall, just below the molding. Then use a piece of cardboard to make the shape of the cornice, including the batten beneath.

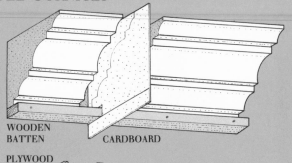

WOODEN BATTEN   CARDBOARD

PLYWOOD

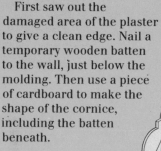

1 *Use the cardboard outline to make a template out of plywood – cutting out the shape with an electric jigsaw. Glue on a triangular block of wood for reinforcement.*

2 *To the template, now screw a baseboard that will fit beneath the batten and touch the wall. Also screw a triangular brace to the back of the template and the baseboard to keep the structure rigid. Then screw a batten to the baseboard each side of the template, immediately behind the allowance for the wall batten: this will allow the template to run along the wall batten.*

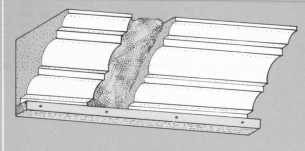

3 *Make a rough filling of the gap with plaster of Paris, reinforcing the layers with jute scrim.*

4 *Gradually add more layers of plaster and run the template along the batten to shape the plaster as it dries.*
You could apply this technique to other damaged plaster – a dado rail, perhaps – but for large areas of damage the molding will have to be prefabricated, off the wall, and fixed later with plaster adhesive.

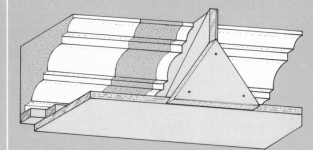

LAYING FLOOR TILES

THE IDEAL BASE FOR a floor of glazed clay is concrete, because the weight of the tiles needs a solid foundation. Always seek advice first if your want to tile over floorboards.

Planning the floor
Unless you mark out the floor first, you will not be able to see how to lay tiles in rooms that are not quite square. Ideally, avoid laying cut tiles that are less than half the full width. Try to run tiles parallel to the longest straight section of a wall. Where the room is not a basic rectangle, align tiles to a focal feature – a fireplace or doorway.

Using battens as guides
The diagrams opposite show how to use battens to keep the tiles at 90° to each other, and level. If the concrete surface is uneven, check that the battens are level, using a spirit level, and use a little mortar mix to prop them if necessary. The tile surface should coincide with the top edge of your battens, allowing for $1/2$ in (1 cm) mortar.

ANGLE GRINDER *for shaving off thin sections from a tile*

Preparing the tiles
The easiest way to cut tiles is to hire a tile cutter. But sometimes you will need to cut the tile at an angle, particularly where a tile needs to taper to fit the edge of the room. Then an angle grinder with a stone disc is the best tool for the job. (Wear goggles and a mask when cutting, because the angle grinder will create thick ceramic dust.) Place a spare strip of tile along the intended line of cut to act as a guide and to prevent the angle grinder from slipping.

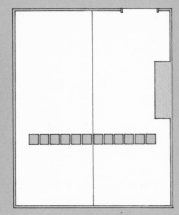

1 *Divide the width of the room into two with a string line, and lay the tiles out from this. If necessary, move the line off-center to ensure that any part-tiles are equal each side of the room. Use strips of hardboard to calculate spaces between the tiles as you lay them out.*

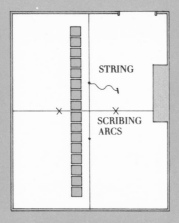

2 *To make a 90° angle from your division line, divide its length in two and then take two points equidistant from the center. Use these as center points for scribing arcs – draw a line between the arcs, giving a 90° angle with the division line. Now calculate the spacing of tiles along the length of the room.*

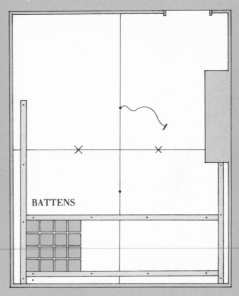

3 *Starting in the corner opposite the doorway, lay two battens at 90° to each other, their edges along the outer edge of the last whole tile. Fix to the concrete with masonry nails. Add a third batten parallel to the first, spaced four tile widths away.*

4 *Cut a leveling board that nearly spans the distance between the outer edges of the parallel battens and notch either end by a tile depth less about $\frac{1}{4}$ in.*

5 *Place sufficient mortar – made from 3 parts builders' sand and 1 part cement – between the battens to provide a base for approximately 20 tiles. Use the notched spreader to level the mortar and dust lightly with dry cement to add a key for the tiles. Place the tiles in position and twist slightly to bed them in. Tap another batten across their surfaces to make sure they are all level. Place spacers between the tiles.*

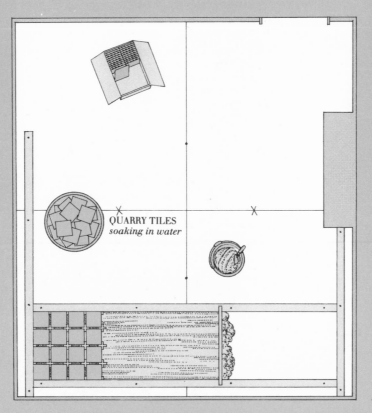

6 *Work in small sections, moving the batten guides as you progress across the room. Do not walk on any freshly laid section for at least 12 hours. When complete, the perimeter battens can be removed and the gaps round the edge of the room filled with tiles that have been cut to fit.*

7 *Grouting can proceed using the same mix of mortar as the bedding, adding a colorizer if desired. In a kitchen it is advisable to use a waterproofing agent in the mortar. Once dry, clean away surplus mortar grout by rubbing the glazed surface with wood shavings and sawdust. Finally, wash the floor with a soapless floor detergent.*

BOXING A RADIATOR

IF YOU PLAN TO HIDE modern radiators in a box, the container must still allow access – so that you can control the thermostatic valve at the side and the bleed valve at the top.

You will also want the radiator to carry on performing its job efficiently – the beading around the edge of the top shelf and the front grill must allow the hot air to escape.

The material for the body of the casing is a high-density building board. It is excellent for cutting and gives a good surface for decoration. Plywood would be equally appropriate, but take care when cutting to avoid broken edges.

Use self-tapping screws (drilling pilot holes if you are using thin board, to prevent the board from splitting).

EXACT DEPTH OF SKIRTING BOARD

1 *Mark out and cut boards for the front and sides of the box, allowing sufficient room for air to circulate around the radiator. Remember to allow for the skirting board on the wall, using a depth gauge to judge its depth and* then cutting off the equivalent from the side pieces of the box. Use an electric jigsaw to cut the boards. Hold up the boards (but don't fix yet) by the radiator to check they fit and still allow space for air circulation.

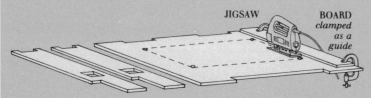

JIGSAW   BOARD clamped as a guide

2 *In the front board, drill holes in each corner and use them as starting points for cutting the hole in which to insert the grill. Clamp a board to the panel to act as a straight guide and cut the hole out with an electrical jigsaw. In the sides, cut access holes so* that you will be able to reach the thermostatic valve. Also cut slots for the air flow at the top and base of the front panel.

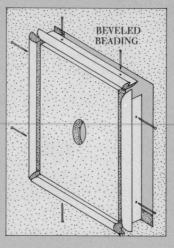

BEVELED BEADING

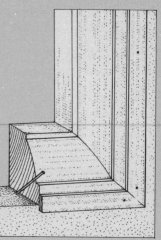

3 *To finish the access hatch hole, cut strips of beveled beading that will fit the space snugly, mitering the corners. Then cut an insert square and glue or nail on the strips to the outer edge of each side. This panel should fit your access hole. Drill a hole in the center to allow you to pull out the panel with your finger. Alternatively, simply nail beading around the hole and leave the space in the middle open.*

4 *Cut lengths of beading to frame the main grill hole, mitering at the corners. Nail into position. Hide any unevenness in the edges of this frame arrow by nailing a narrow, flat beading strip over the join between the frame beading and the edge of the front board.*

5 *Cut out the grill panel with tin cutters. If you want to paint the grill, do it before adding it to the box, so you can hold the grill flat.*

Screw flat beading to the edges of the grill – this holds the grill in position – then screw the entire grill panel to the back of the framing beading that was fitted, around the edges of the hole in the front board.

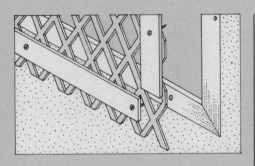

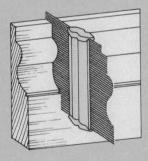

WOODEN TRIANGLE

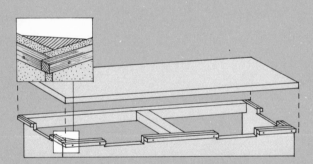

6 *Fit and screw the front and sides of the radiator box together. To strengthen the unit, nail a strip of wood to the back, a cross brace in the center, and glue small wooden triangles at the corners.*

7 *To allow air flow, screw on small strips of wood to the outer edges of the box. Cut a lid from 1 in (25 mm) thick board to the size of the outer edge of the small sections of wood.*

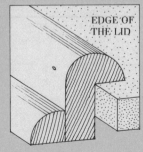

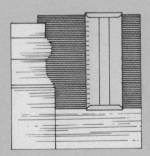

8 *Add skirting board to the bottom of the box; remember to allow for air flow. Use a profile gauge to transfer the pattern of the skirting on the wall to the new skirting board. Use a coping saw to achieve a perfect fit.*

EDGE OF THE LID

CORNER BEADING

9 *Add the finishing touches: beading along the edge of the lid will prevent the lid sliding – it needs to be at least 1 in (25 mm) deep to hide the frame and air flow gap; and add beading to the corners of the box for a classic finish.*

BOXING A BATHTUB

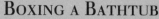

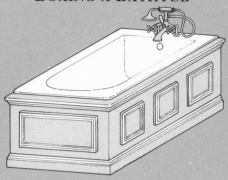

IF YOU WANT TO BOX in a roll-top cast iron bathtub, you need to create a simple frame and allow an access hatch to the plumbing. This frame can be built around a bathtub that is positioned against two walls; you can also apply the same technique to make a supplementary frame for molded plastic bathtubs. However, never use the frame to replace one specifically made to support the flexible structure of plastic bathtubs.

The frame is of 2×2 in (50×50 mm) sawed softwood, with glued and screwed lap joints where necessary. The sides are covered with high density building board, with a paneled effect that is made by using softwood molding. The surrounding shelf is made from 1×4 in (25×100 mm) board with a rounded facing edge. You can add architrave molding beneath the shelf and skirting board at the bottom of the panels.

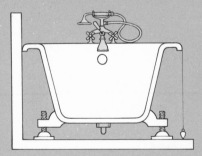

1 *Mark out the exact position of the outside rim of the bathtub on the floor, using a plumb line from several points around its edge. The frame will fit along the inside of the line you draw on the floor.*

2 Measure and cut the lengths necessary to build the basic frame. Do not assume that the verticals are all the same length: take individual measurements to be sure there will be a tight fit between the bathtub lip and the shelf. Without a tight fit, splashed water, sitting on the shelf may seep between the join and cause rot. Remember that your vertical measurement needs to account for the depth of the shelf.

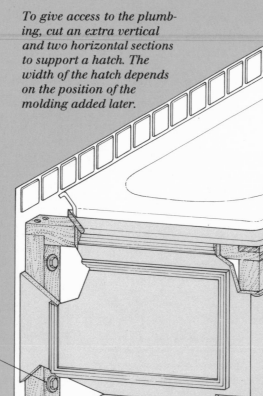

As an EXPANSION BOLT is tightened a segmented metal shell expands to grip the hole tightly.

To give access to the plumbing, cut an extra vertical and two horizontal sections to support a hatch. The width of the hatch depends on the position of the molding added later.

ACCESS HATCH

3 Before fixing, check the frame fits around the bathtub. Note that the timber frame sections that support the access hatch are simply jointed into the main frame (in shallow through-housings) and are skew-nailed together (see page 163). The middle of the lower horizontal cross brace in the hatch should be level with the top of the skirting board you will add later.

4 The final position of the shelf in relation to the frame depends on the amount of overhang you need – to cover the side panel, the decorative architrave molding you add later, and a little extra depth if you want the shelf to be a feature.
   Cut the shelf, mitering the corner at 45°. Mark the line of the frame along the underside of the shelf, so that the shelf can be re-positioned correctly once the frame is fitted around the bathtub.

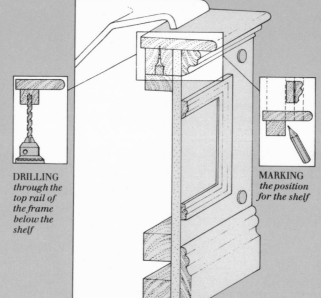

DRILLING through the top rail of the frame below the shelf

MARKING the position for the shelf

5 Screw the sections of the frame together. To fix the verticals that butt up against the wall, use either hammer plugs or small wall expansion bolts. Drill straight through the frame and into the wall with a masonry bit. Screw the lower horizontal sections into the floor, but take care not to penetrate deeper than the depth of floorboards – usually $^3/_4$ in (18 mm).

6 Place the shelf in position, using the guideline. Glue the mitered corner together. Use a dowel bit to drill 1 in (25 mm) holes into the underside of the top of the frame, leaving no more than 18 in (45 cm) between each hole. Through the center of each hole drill a pilot hole up into the shelf. Screw the shelf to the frame.

7 *Measure and cut the side panels from high density building board. Cut the long side as one piece from end to end, but cut it again, vertically, where it coincides with the vertical support for the access hatch. Then cut the smaller section into three: the top strip will be the same depth as the architrave molding and fits behind it; the center piece is the access panel itself; the bottom section is the same height as the skirting board and fits behind that.*

8 *Lay all the boards for the side panels on the floor and mark the positions for the molding. Cut lengths of softwood molding, miter corners at 45° and glue and pin in position.*

Nail the side panels to the frame, using lost-headed nails – punch home and back-fill with wood filler. Use screws for the access panel, so that it can be removed as necessary (the screw heads can be disguised with plastic screw covers).

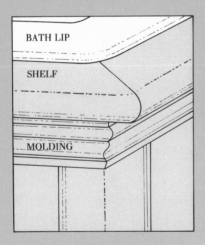

9 *As final decorative touches, fix architrave molding around the top of the panels, beneath the shelf, and skirting board around the bottom of the panels, mitering corners at 45°. Also add a length of corner-angle molding to cover the sharp edge of the corner between the top molding and the skirting board. The completed box can be painted, perhaps picking out the panel sections or the molding in different colors.*

ORNATE VALANCE

PICTURE FRAME molding – either bought new or recycled from an old frame – makes a theatrical valance over a window. It will look spectacular if it is heavily gilded or painted with a bravura finish.

Before you fix the valance to the wall, decide whether you want to drape material over the valance – the bracket holding the valance to the wall will need to provide a gap for this.

1 *Measure the length of molding you need for your window and cut each end at 45°. Position the molding above the window, then using a spirit level (or, in an older dwelling, following the picture rail, cornices or lintel, if they exist) lightly mark the position of the valance on the wall above the window.*

3 *Mark the position for each bracket on the valance by holding the valance up against the brackets on the wall. Screw brackets to the valance. If the valance is particularly deep, then it will need support lower down too. Take small blocks of wood and drill a hole in each, the same diameter as a piece of dowel. Glue a length of dowel (the same depth as the brackets) in each block and then glue the blocks to the valance.*

4 *To fix the valance to the wall brackets, sit the valance brackets on top of those on the wall and pass short, slotted bolts through from below. Tighten up with nuts, using pliers or a small wrench.*

2 *Position your first set of angle brackets on the wall and secure – use a masonry bit to drill into the wall and insert wall plugs to take screws. Use as many brackets as the weight of your valance demands: molding from an old frame can often be very heavy and will need support at regular intervals along the whole of its length.*

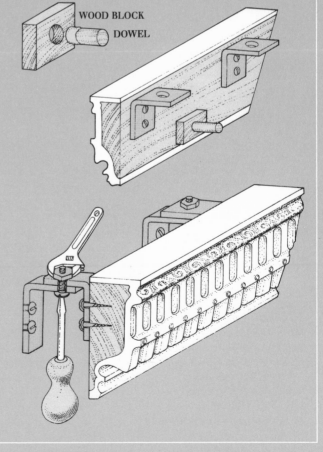

FURNITURE TECHNIQUES

TURNING A TRAY INTO A TABLE

A LIGHTWEIGHT, folding base is perfect to transform a large and solid tray into an occasional table. You could decorate a plain, wooden tray to match the legs, so that you have what appears to be one piece of furniture. It's easiest to decorate the legs before they are assembled.

Use a hardwood like cherry or mahogany for the frames – you may need to visit a timber specialist for this. Ask for a planed finish of 2×1 in (50×25 mm) and 2×2 in (50×50 mm).

It's a good idea to draw up a full-scale plan of the legs to ensure that the angle at which the legs meet the floor is correct. This angle is determined by the breadth of the wooden rim that you will fix to the underside of the tray to keep it in position on the legs (minus $\frac{1}{2}$ in (1 cm) leeway each side so that the fit of the tray on the legs is not too tight).

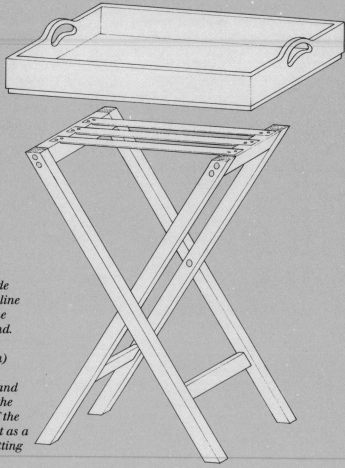

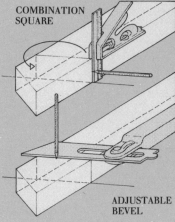

1 Turn the tray upside down and mark a line $\frac{1}{4}$ in (6 mm) in from the edge, all the way around. Make up a frame from $\frac{1}{2} \times \frac{1}{2}$ in (12×12 mm) square section wood, mitered at the corners and glued into position on the tray along the inside of the line. This frame will act as a position guide when setting down the tray.

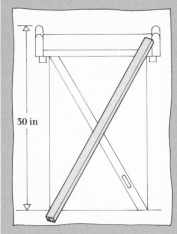

2 Ideally, the top of the tray should be no higher than 30 in (75 cm) off the floor. Use lengths of 2×1 in (50×25 mm) timber for the legs. Lay one length on your plan drawing and mark up the angles of both ends with a combination square and adjustable bevel. Once you have cut one leg to the correct length, use it as a template for the other three.

COMBINATION SQUARE

ADJUSTABLE BEVEL

3 These four pieces will make two sets of legs that will fit inside each other. At exactly the mid-point between the top and bottom of the inner legs, mark the position for a pivot hole, match the two legs up and drill through both. If possible, use a drill mounted in a stand to ensure a perfect hole. Match the size of the hole to the diameter of a good quality hardwood dowel. Use each of the inner legs as a guide for its neighboring outer leg, but drill only part of the way through the outer leg (the dowel will not go right through the outer legs).

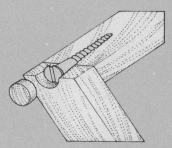

4 Drill out two holes at the top of each leg, $\frac{1}{4}$ in (6 mm) deep. These holes will take lengths of dowel that will disguise the heads of screws – the screws are used to fix the legs to the top cross braces (step 7).

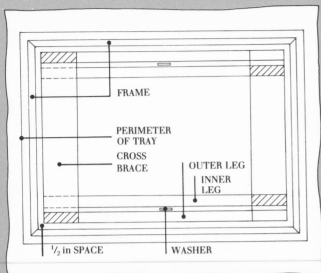

FRAME

PERIMETER
OF TRAY

CROSS
BRACE

OUTER LEG

INNER
LEG

$^1/_2$ in SPACE

WASHER

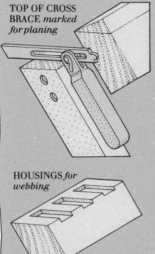

TOP OF CROSS
BRACE *marked
for planing*

HOUSINGS *for
webbing*

FOLDING SCREEN

5 *Make yourself a plan to work out the measurement of the top cross braces. Cut two lengths of 2 × 2 in (50 × 50 mm) timber for the top cross braces, allowing about $^1/_2$ in (1 cm) inside the rim on the tray, so the tray can fit loosely on top of the legs. The inner legs will need a shorter cross brace; remember to allow for a thin steel washer that will fit between the legs at the pivot point.*

6 *Using an adjustable bevel, take the angle of the top of one leg and mark it on the ends of the top cross braces. Support the cross braces in a bench vice and plane the top side to the line you marked. Measure out the width of your webbing and mark equal spaces between each strip on the top of each brace. Cut end housings to take the webbing – stop short of the total width, so that the ends are not visible.*

T HE STYLE OF SCREEN you want to make will depend on the use you envision for it – in the Orient the screen is a decorative object in its own right, while the West treats a screen more as a showcase for decoration, such as montage, painting on canvas or tapestry.

Suitable materials

Hardwood is especially suitable for tall, elegant panels. The panel frames of a 5–7 ft (1.5–2 m) screen will need cross-braces of at least 2 × 1 in (50 × 25 mm) wood. Ask to have frame lengths machine-mitered, so that the corners will be very neat and accurate. Depending on the frame's thickness, it can be glued and then either screwed or nailed together at the corners.

Use simple picture-frame moldings around the panels, to give the screen a solid look. There are various finishing touches worth trying – liming oak, polishing mahogany, or extending the decorative image in the panels to include the frame area.

The three sections of this screen illustrate different techniques of construction, to support alternative forms of decoration. The central panel has an elegant curved top (as does the screen decorated on page 137) to break up the angularity of the lines.

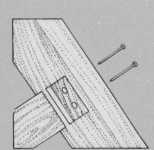

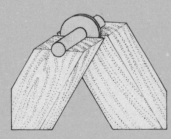

9 *Cut webbing to span the two cross braces. Fix one end of the central length of webbing in its housing with tacks; hold the other end in position on the opposite cross brace. Place the tray on the base to find the correct point for fixing the unattached end of webbing – remember to allow the $^1/_2$ in (1 cm) clearance each side. Then cut and tack the remaining lengths of webbing in place.*

7 *Cut lower cross braces, allowing $^1/_4$ in (6 mm) extra each end so that they can fit in shallow housings in the legs. Fit these cross braces into the legs and fix with glue and lost-head nails – drill pilot holes first so the wood does not split.*

Fix the top braces with glue and screws.

8 *Fit the two sets of legs inside each other and join together using hardwood dowel as pivots in the central holes. The dowel slides in through its hole on the inner leg, through a thin steel washer (which prevents the legs rubbing together) and finally into the outer leg (fix it here with wood glue).*

HANGING, *on hardboard*

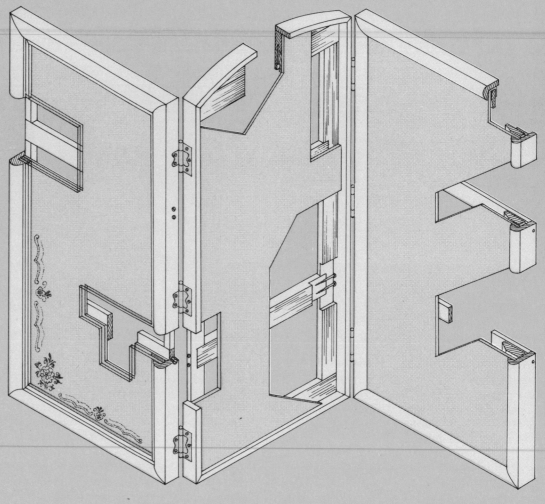

Panel for hangings
This frame design is ideal for delicate embroidered hangings. Its construction is very similar to that of a large picture frame, using deeply-rebated molding with a gently curved face.

1 Decide on the height and width of the screen and make up the frame. Slot in a gilded wood fillet, the hanging supported on a sheet of hardboard (if it is a delicate embroidery, attach it with Velcro as described on page 180), and protect the hanging with a sheet of clear plastic if necessary.

2 Position horizontal cross braces made out of 3 × 1 in (75 × 25 mm) at one-third intervals to strengthen the screen. Fix the cross braces with brass screws, counter-sunk into the sides of the frame.

3 Finally, to keep the edges of the panel flat, insert lengths of square section beading between the cross-braces. Fix in place with panel pins.

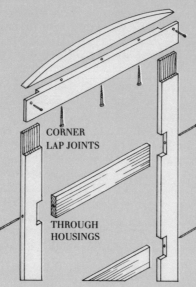

CORNER LAP JOINTS

THROUGH HOUSINGS

Hardboard panel
Use 2 × 1 in (50 × 25 mm) softwood to make a frame with two verticals and four horizontals. Fix the top and bottom corners with corner lap joints; space the remaining horizontals at one-third intervals and fix in through-housings.

1 Glue and screw all the joints together. To fix the curved top section, drill through half the depth of the horizontal brace below. Run a pilot hole through the remaining section and up into the curved top. Glue before screwing together.

2 Cut hardboard to fit the frame. Glue together the common surface areas and fix with copper-coated panel pins. If you want to paint the panel, prime the surface first, or use oil-tempered hardboard.
After painting, nail on a surrounding strip of about 2 × 1 in (50 × 25 mm) , mitered at the corners. If you find that the strip will not bend to match the curved top, then cut shallow, closely-spaced grooves across the underside, midway along the strip. Fill the grooves with woodfiller where they are visible.

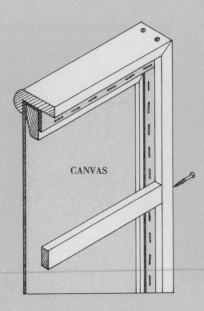

CANVAS

KITCHEN WORKSTAND

Canvas panel
In the final variation, the panel is a traditional canvas mounted stretcher (as would be used by an artist). You can paint a design on the canvas with oil or acrylic paints.

1 *Stretcher timber is sold to the nearest centimeter or inch. Make up the stretcher to screen proportions, and then stretch the canvas tightly but evenly over the edges and staple to the back, taking care that the canvas is free of wrinkles.*

2 *Make up a surrounding frame for the finished artwork panel, similar to the frame for the first panel of this screen. However, the frame need not be so heavy because the stretcher is a self-supporting unit.*

3 *To hold the stretcher in place, you need only two 2 × 1 in (50 × 25 mm) cross braces. Fix these in the same way as the cross braces that were fixed in the first panel.*

Completing the screen
Once you have made three similar panels, complete the screen by fixing the panels together with hinges.

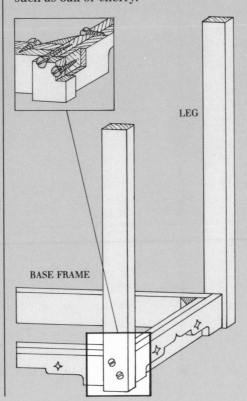

LEG

BASE FRAME

A TOUCH OF THEATRICALITY disguises the simple joinery in this workstand, which is really a form of glorified shelving. As a piece of country furniture, the wood will look most convincing if the finish is quite rough, rather than highly polished: Look for old floorboards in hardwoods such as oak or cherry.

The overall length and breadth of the workstand will depend on the space available. But to make the tiling simpler, it is convenient if the depth does not exceed that of three 6 in (150 mm) square ceramic tiles (including grouting), plus the surrounding woodwork – approximately 22 in (55 cm) in all.

1 *This workstand fits together in three layers. The area below the bottom shelf is the base. Cut 6 × 1 in (150 × 25 mm) boards that overlap each other to make a firm frame. Cut out the pattern on the outer boards with a jigsaw. Screw the inner boards to the outer, so no fixings are visible on the outside face. Glue in corner braces, to keep the base square.*

2 *Decide on the finished height of the tiled surface. Use 3 × 1 in (75 × 25 mm) timber for the legs at the corners and 2 × 1 in (50 × 25 mm) for the inside legs. The legs at the rear should be cut longer so that they can support the frame that surrounds the row of upright tiles at the back of the workstand. Allow extra length at this stage anyway, as the waste can be trimmed later.*
    Fix the legs to the base by screwing through the front face. The screw heads will be hidden beneath the decorative strips that are added later.

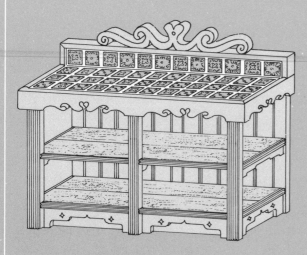

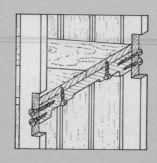

6 *Nail the bottom shelf to the base. Divide the distance between the bottom shelf and the underside of the decorative skirting to determine the position of the middle shelf. Cut three 2 × 2 in (50 × 50 mm) cross braces to support the middle shelf and cut out a shallow pattern to echo that beneath the bottom shelf. Fix in position by nailing through the legs (make pilot holes first). Screw the boards to the cross braces from the underside.*

3 *For the top surface use blockboard at least 1 in (25 mm) deep. From the front edge only cut out housings equal to the depth of the front legs. Check the surface is level all round, then screw all the legs to the blockboard.*

4 *Cut out a decorative fascia for the front and sides to hide the joint between the tiles, top surface and legs. Draw out the pattern to be cut away – use a jigsaw to remove the accessible areas of waste and a coping saw for the difficult areas. The corners should be mitered at 45°.*

The fascia is positioned so the top edge exceeds the top of the blockboard surface by the equivalent of a tile's depth. Glue and nail the skirting in position.

5 *Measure and cut boards for the shelves. Remember the shelves are housed around the front legs – the depth of housing must also allow for the depth of a decorative strip that will be added to the leading edge of the shelves later (step 9). This strip will then be flush with the front of the legs.*

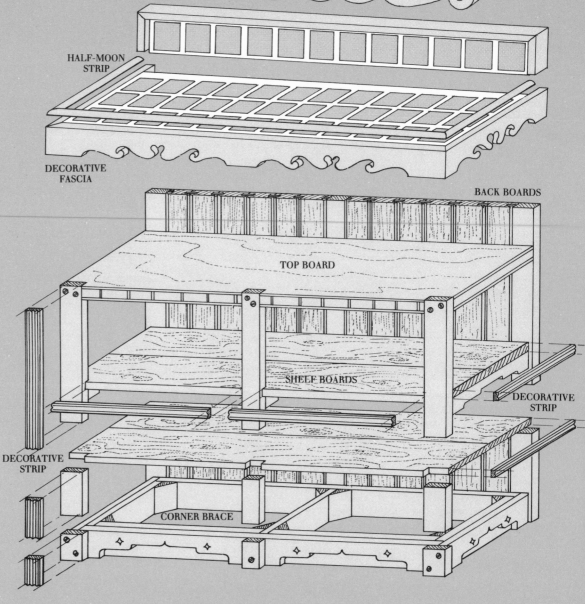

HALF-MOON STRIP

DECORATIVE FASCIA

BACK BOARDS

TOP BOARD

DECORATIVE STRIP

SHELF BOARDS

DECORATIVE STRIP

CORNER BRACE

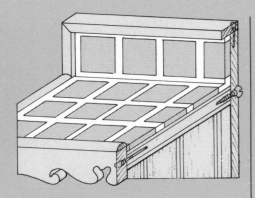

From Chest of Drawers to Dresser

IT IS RELATIVELY SIMPLE to transform a chest of drawers into a kitchen dresser – shelves are added above and the whole unit is decorated to look like an integrated piece of furniture. If the chest of drawers is particularly fine wood – such as mahogany – then ideally the shelf section should be made in hardwood to match.

Dimensions and proportions need to be carefully calculated to achieve a balance between the top and bottom units. A recommended minimum timber depth is $7/8$ in (22.5 mm); allow up to $1 1/8$ in (30 mm) if you need a more weighty look. Remember also to research the distances between shelves – it is easy to misjudge the ratio between them.

A dresser can become top heavy with china, so to achieve stability the base of the shelf unit should be housed in the top surface of the chest of drawers. If you are loathe to cut into the surface of the chest, consider fixing the shelf unit to the wall with mirror plates. To add strength to the shelves, secure them to the side boards of the unit in stopped housings – these will also disguise the ends of the shelves.

7 *Now make up a frame surround for the vertical tiles, using strips of 2 × 1 in (50 × 25 mm). The height needs to be measured from the level of the blockboard surface with an allowance for the depth of one horizontal and one vertical tile, plus grouting. The front face of the frame will match the depth of the top edge of the decorative skirting. Miter the two corners and then glue and nail them together. Once set, hold the frame in position and trim the legs to that they touch the underside of the frame. Nail the frame to the legs.*

8 *Fill in the space between the back legs and the frame with old matchboard or boards similar to those used for the shelves. Fix them to the frame by nailing through the top of the frame and into the end-grain of the boards. Screw through the boards where they meet the shelves and along the base board.*

9 *Add a half-moon strip to the top edge of the decorative skirting. Cut lengths of fluted molding strip for the front legs and the edges and ends of each shelf. Fix with panel pins.*

10 *Grout the tiles in position on the top surface. The vertical ones will need spacers for support until they set. Use an acrylic grout if the surface is likely to get wet regularly. Finally, fix a carved top piece, if possible echoing the cutout pattern on the decorative fascia below.*

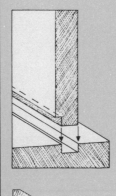

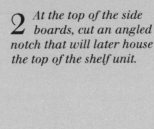

1 *For the sides of the shelf unit, cut two identical boards – to a length that you decide will be adequate to accommodate three shelves. At the base of each side cut out a rebate along the inner (shelf) face. This rebate should be about $1/3$– $1/2$ the total thickness of the board. It should have a*

2 *At the top of the side boards, cut an angled notch that will later house the top of the shelf unit.*

depth of about $3/8$–$1/2$ in (9–12 mm); this depth will match the stopped housing that is later cut out of the top of the chest of drawers (in step 7 – cut these housings only after the shelf unit is assembled: their position is related to the length of the shelf unit and needs to be very accurate).

3 *On each side board also mark the positions of the $1/4$ in (6 mm) deep stopped housings for the shelves. The housings are set back $1/2$ in (12 mm) from the front face of the board and at the rear by the depth of the back panel. Cut the housings with a router or spade bit and chisel.*

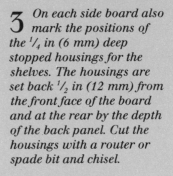

If you want to stain the top unit to give it a more natural and even appearance, do so before assembling – it is difficult to rub stain into tight corners. If the back panel is to be made from new tongue-and-groove boards, remember that shrinkage will expose the tongues, so paint or stain these surfaces as well, before fixing them together.

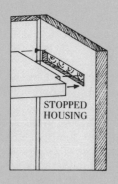

STOPPED HOUSING

4 Although the depth of each shelf differs, they all fit flush with the front of the side boards. At the rear they match the end of the stopped housings in the sides, to allow for the back panel. Cut the shelves and remove a notch from the front edge of each end, so that the shelf will fit tightly into its housing.

5 Mark the location of all the shelf housings on the outer face of the sideboards. Using a dowel bit, drill $\frac{1}{4}$ in (6 mm) deep holes where each screw will go. Glue the shelves in their housings and drill pilot holes in the center of each dowel hole as a guide for the screws. Screw through the side boards into the shelves and hide the heads with $\frac{1}{4}$ in (6 mm) lengths of dowel, glued in position.

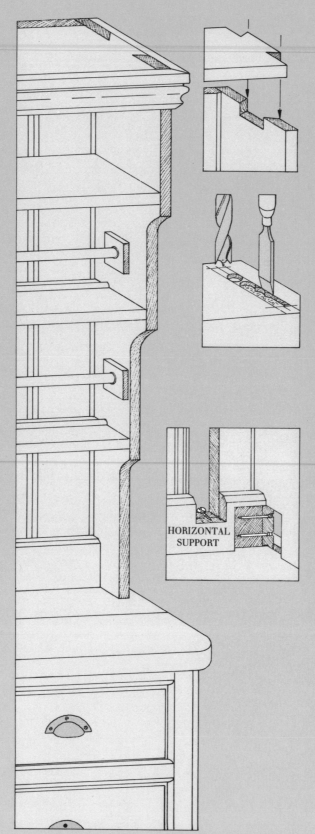

HORIZONTAL SUPPORT

6 Cut a length of timber to form the top of the shelf unit. Cut notches to correspond with those cut in the top of the side boards, so forming an angled lap joint that will hold the top securely. Glue and nail into place.

7 As the length of the shelf unit can now be measured, mark out and cut the stopped housings in the top surface of the chest of drawers. An accurate fit is needed, so that the shelves are held firmly in place.
  To cut a stopped housing use a router or wide diameter drill bit supported by a drill stand. The remaining waste can be accurately removed with a firmer chisel.

8 For the back panel, try to use old, wide tongue-and-groove or lapped boards. If an even number will not fit across the width of the unit, cut equal amounts from the two boards at each end. Screw the boards to the back of the shelves, checking that the shelves and the side boards remain square on.

9 The back boards will need a horizontal support along the bottom: this will also neaten the appearance of the unit. Cut a length of 3×1 in (75×25 mm) and plane a bevel along the top front edge. Place it in position against the back panel and drive nails through the side boards into the end grain. Finally, screw the boards to this support from behind.
  If the unit has to take a lot of weight, attach a couple of brass mirror plates to span the join between the back of the top and bottom units.

10 Add horizontal lengths of dowel to keep precious plates in position. Using a spade bit, drill a hole in a flat, square section of wood, to the diameter of the dowel. Insert the dowel in each support and secure it in the shelf using panel pins. Then pin a section of small-gauge quadrant beading along the shelves at the point where the plates sit.

FABRIC TECHNIQUES

COVERING A CHEST

TRANSFORM THE PLAINEST of chests into a seat, using padding and a fabric covering. Before you begin, remove the lid from its hinges.

To pad the lid, use upholstery wadding, building up layers to make a soft seat. Cut rectangles of padding, allowing ¼ in (6 mm) extra all around on the top layers for a firmly-padded look. The sides can either be simply covered with fabric, or have a layer of wadding too – cut rectangles to size. Or you could paint the sides, echoing the pattern and the colors of the fabric on the lid.

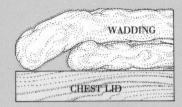

1 *Stick layers of wadding to the lid with latex adhesive, building up a domed look by putting slightly smaller rectangles of wadding beneath the main rectangles.*

2 *Cut a rectangle of fabric that will fit over the lid, allowing enough overlap for it to be tacked to the inside of the lid. Cut rectangles of fabric for each side, allowing extra so that the fabric will overlap the corners and the top and bottom of the chest.*

3 *Cover the wadding on the lid with fabric material, folding over the edges of the fabric to the inside of the lid. Turn the lid over and begin fixing the fabric with upholstery tacks, starting at the center of each side. Then add more tacks, checking that the fabric stays taut.*

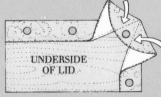

4 *At the corners, cut away the surplus fabric and fold the corners together to meet at 45°, tacking the folds in place.*

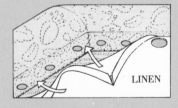

5 *To give a neat finish inside the lid, cut a piece of linen and fold in its edges ½ in (12 mm) all round. Tack the linen neatly round the inside of the lid, covering the raw edges of the main fabric.*

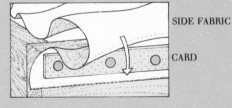

6 *Now fix the side pieces of fabric. To hide the tacks at the top of each side, back-tack: cut four strips of strong card to fit the width of each side, position one side covering with its wrong side uppermost and tack it with three or four tacks to keep it in place, then tack the card along the top of the side.*

7 *Fix any wadding in position on the sides of the chest with latex adhesive, then fold the fabric down over the card, so that the tacks are hidden. Tack the other end of the fabric on to the bottom of the chest, folding under the edges of the fabric first.*

8 *Miter the corner joins on the base and tack the sides of the fabric round the corners to the nearby sides of the chest. Repeat the same process with the opposite side. Then fix the tops of the remaining two sides of fabric; fold in the sides of these pieces at the corners, pin temporarily in place, then slip-stitch for a neat finish.*

9 *Finally, add wooden feet or castors, so that the fabric tacked to the base of the chest is protected from wear. Replace the lid on to its hinges.*

CARPET CHAIR COVER

A PARTLY WORN-OUT carpet or kilim with mellow colors can be put to use as a chair covering. Use the sound pieces from the carpet, bearing in mind the amount of weight it needs to carry. Designs of chair like the one in this picture are quite common, but you could make a similar cover for an old rocking chair or a folding director's chair.

1 *Measure the area of the back and seat – remember to allow for the material that has to wrap around the front and rear cross struts of the seat. Cut equivalent pieces from the carpet, matching the pattern in both pieces if possible.*

2 *Position the carpet on the chair back with a few temporary upholstery tacks. Then fix with permanent tacks, starting in the center of each side and working outwards. Ease out the temporary tacks with a tack lifter. To hide the tacks, stick a length of braid with latex adhesive, securing with gimp pins or decorative nails.*

3 *On the seat, wrap the carpet around the front and rear cross braces and fold back to prevent fraying (if you find the carpet a bit too thick for this, try shaving off some of the pile). Insert a narrow gauge steel rod (available from hardware stores or blacksmiths) along the length of this fold – this eases the pressure. Then tack the carpet to the wooden struts, close to the steel rod.*
   Tack the sides of the carpet to the sides of the chair and cover the edges with braid.

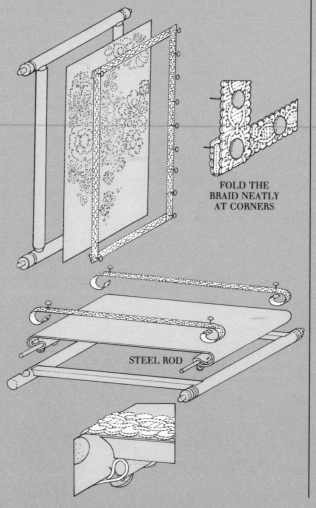

FOLD THE
BRAID NEATLY
AT CORNERS

STEEL ROD

HAND-HOOKED RUG

Y OU NEED ONLY the most basic equipment to make a colorful hooked rug. The backing should be an even, fairly open weave mixture of cotton and linen – this will work better than the traditional hessian.
   Use thin strips of cloth for the yarn, cut from fabric oddments. You will also need a hand hook to pull strips through the backing.

HAND HOOK

1 *Draw out your design on graph paper first. You may find following the design easier if you mark it on the backing fabric with a felt-tipped pen. Traditionally, these rugs have naive, often animal designs, and use bold slabs of color.*

2 *Prepare the strips of fabric – remove any buttons, open up any seams, and wash the fabric. Cut the fabric into strips, $^1/_8$–$^1/_2$ in (3–12 mm) wide. The thinner the width of the strips, the finer the rug will be. Cut woven fabrics along the grain and knitted fabrics along their length.*

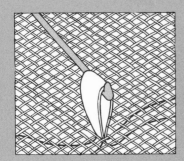

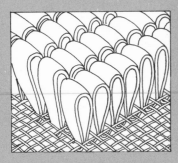

Cushion Covers

3 *With the backing fabric face up, hold a strip of fabric beneath. Insert the hook through the backing and pull the strip of fabric through from the underside to form a loop.*

Continue by moving the hook forward a few backing threads and pulling through another loop. Start and finish a length of yarn by pulling the ends through to the top of the rug.

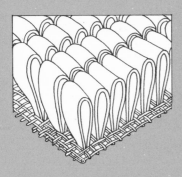

4 *To make a neat edge, fold the edges of the backing fabric over to the right side to make a hem of about 1 in (25 mm), aligning the weave. Then pull the yarn through both thicknesses. To give the edge extra strength, sew a strip of rug binding over the back of the hem.*

A SQUARE CUSHION COVER is simple to make and offers endless scope for using fabrics and different edgings. Try using more unusual fabrics – a cover made from a piece of old tapestry, perhaps with tassels at each corner, will have a rich, Gothic air.

2 IN SEAM

OPENING TACKED TOGETHER

2 IN SEAM

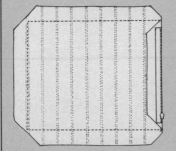

Always make a cover to fit over a cushion pad, rather than putting loose fillings straight in the cover, so that the cover can be removed and cleaned. For plump cushions, cut out the cover the same size as the pad without allowing extra for the seams.

1 *Measure the size of the cushion pad and cut out two squares of fabric to fit, adding an extra $^5/_8$ in (15 mm) all round for the seams.*

2 *Place the cushion back and front together, their right sides facing. Stitch seams for about 2 in (50 mm) from both ends of one edge, leaving the center open for a zipper. Tack the center of this seam allowance together and press the whole seam open. Pin the zipper face down over the seam and tack. Stitch in place from the right side.*

3 *Stitch around the other three edges of the cover. Trim the seam allowance at the corners. Neaten the raw edges with machine zigzag stitch.*

4 *Turn the cover to the right side, pulling out the corners if necessary with a pin. Press the cover. Handstitch a fringe to the sides, or decorative tassels to the corners.*

DISPLAY TECHNIQUES

HANGING A QUILT

QUILTS — ESPECIALLY OLD quilts — are delicate articles. Because they are made up of thousands of interlocking threads, they are especially vulnerable to gravitational force: hung from one side alone, a quilt will be irreparably pulled out of shape. Instead, its weight needs to be evenly spread around all its four sides.

The answer is to make a frame to which you fix strips of Velcro; you can then hang the quilt just as if it is a picture to make an effective wall display. You can use the same technique for hanging a tapestry or embroidery, or you could hang these – still using the Velcro technique – in the panel of a screen (see page 172).

Hanging a quilt on a frame will prevent it being pulled out of shape from the top, but it is still a good idea to take it down at least once a year to let the fabric rest. Fold the quilt and store it horizontally – hang another quilt or picture in its place.

It is possible to staple strips of Velcro directly on to some walls, but these will look unsightly when you want to remove the quilt – a frame is much more versatile and can be simply exchanged if you decide to replace one quilt with another.

If the quilt is particularly old or fragile, seek expert advice first from a conservator about giving it extra support for hanging.

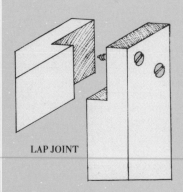

LAP JOINT

1 *For the backing, either use an artist's canvas stretcher, cut to size, or make up a frame using lengths of 2 × 1 in (50 × 25 mm) planed softwood, lap-jointing the corners. Use hardwood if the frame is going to be visible.*

2 *Staple lengths of ½ in (12 mm) Velcro all round the front face of the frame or the stretcher.*

3 *Cut 6 in (150 mm) lengths of Velcro and slip stitch carefully to the back of the quilt, round the edges near the binding. Leave a gap of 2 in (50 mm) between each strip of Velcro but make sure each corner has a strip attached.*

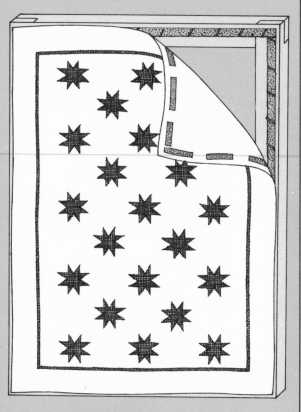

4 *Press the Velcro on the quilt against that on the frame. The whole unit can then be hung on the wall – attach screw eyes to the back of the frame and tie on nylon cord.*

PICTURE FRAME

FOR A PROFESSIONAL JOB it is worth investing in a steel miter block (for perfect 45° mitered joints), a miter rule and precision cutter.

Remember that the inner dimensions of the frame surrounding the artwork mount differ considerably from the outer edges. Also allow an extra ¹/₁₆ in leeway on the dimensions of the artwork mount when you mark up the molding.

1 *After marking up, cut out the frame lengths on the miter block. If you have a long, awkward length of molding, first cut it down into smaller sections, otherwise it can twist.*

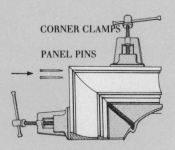

CORNER CLAMPS

PANEL PINS

2 *Glue and clamp the lengths together. A set of miter clamps will work better than other types of frame clamps, which restrict access to the corners. To avoid dents or scratches, take care to spread the pressure of the clamps, cushioning with off-cuts of wood, card or cloth.*

3 Nail long panel pins through each corner to strengthen the joints. To prevent the wood from splitting, use the sharp point of a compass to make a pilot hole for the pins. Use a fine gauge nail punch to push the heads just below the surface of the wood – or use a masonry nail with its point filed down.

4 Once the glue has set, release the frame from the clamps. Add any decorative finish at this stage, while all surfaces are still accessible.

5 Ask a glazier to cut a sheet of picture glass to size. Position the glass inside the frame and tape the gap between the glass and frame. Take care that the tape does not encroach on the glass where it could be visible from the front side. The tape will prevent dirt, dust and tiny insects from entering. Self-adhesive tape, such as masking tape, is not suitable for framing or conservation jobs because it will dry out and fall off – use only plain brown paper tape that sticks when it is wetted.

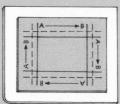

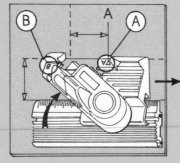

6 Draw up the width of mount to surround the picture area on the reverse side of a piece of acid-free, 6-ply mounting board. Draw a line exactly 1 in (25 mm) inside the first line and allow the corners to intersect. Use a precision board cutter to cut the mount: insert the cutter in its groove on the precision ruler and place the measuring edge along the innermost line. Run the cutter between points A and B (see left), which are aligned with arrows A and B on the cutter.

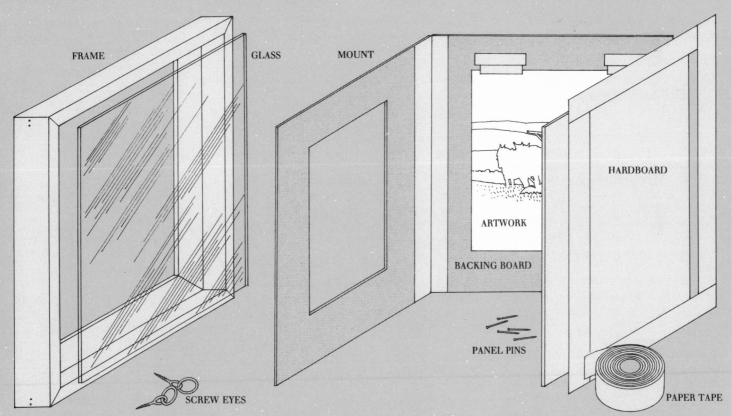

FRAME   GLASS   MOUNT

HARDBOARD

ARTWORK

BACKING BOARD

PANEL PINS

SCREW EYES

PAPER TAPE

7 Use the mount as a template to cut a backing card for the artwork (use a minimum 2-ply card; it must be acid-free, otherwise it will damage watercolors and prints). Join the mount and backing card along one edge with linen tape and an animal glue adhesive, or use paper tape.

8 Attach the top of the artwork to the backing card with strips of plain brown paper tape. This forms a hinge from which the artwork hangs free to allow for expansion and contraction.

9 Finally, to protect the artwork and mounts, insert a good quality hardboard backing that allows a little room for expansion. This is held in position with non-corrosive pins and sealed with paper tape. Then fix screw eyes into the back of the frame to take wire or nylon cord.

GLOSSARY

A

AMISH PEOPLE – members of the most conservative sect of the U.S. and Canadian Mennonite church among whom nearly all kinds of decoration are forbidden. Patchwork quilts are allowed because they serve a practical purpose and are usually made in geometric designs from somber, solid colors, relieved by small pieces of brightly colored, contrasting fabric

ANAGLYPHIC (trademark) – type of thick, embossed wallpaper

APPLIQUÉ – textile technique in which pieces of fabric are cut out and fixed, usually by needlework, on top of a larger and different background fabric

ARCHITRAVE – decorative molded frame that surrounds a wall panel, doorway or window opening

ARMOIRE – large, heavy ornamental cupboard with two doors, originally built to keep weapons but now used to store clothes.

ART DECO – 1930s modernist style of art inspired by mechanical forms and chiefly distinguished by geometrical shapes, bold color schemes and symmetrical designs, suitable for mass production

ART NOUVEAU – style of art and architecture, popular in the 1890s, that intended to break with the rigid classicism of the past. Opalescent colors are coupled with the ornate swaying curves of stylized natural forms, especially plants, hair and waves, to create well-crafted, asymmetrical designs

ARTS AND CRAFTS MOVEMENT – late Victorian country-based movement, inspired by William Morris's socialist principles, that advocated a return to traditional handcrafts and which produced solid but somber furniture

AUBUSSON – town in France, renowned for its tapestry factories which produced flat-woven carpets in large numbers in the nineteenth century, marked by their symmetrical designs, classical decorations and soft colors

AUSTRIAN BLIND – full blind that draws up into loops of fabric

B

BALUSTER – turned, upright post, usually with a swollen base and a narrow neck, that provides support for a rail and collectively forms a balustrade

BALUSTRADE – ornamental rail with a supporting row of balusters, used to contain staircases and balconies

BARGELLO – needlework technique, mainly used for upholstery, in which each element of the design uses a single color of differing tones.

BEADING – slender, cylindrical molding, sometimes resembling a row of beads, that is used for edging or ornamentation

BOLSTER – long, narrow pillow or cushion that constitutes an essential part of a chair, sofa or bed

C

CABRIOLE – curved style of furniture leg, popular in the early eighteenth century, that bends out distinctively at the knee, tapers inwards again after it and ends in an upturned foot

CALICO – coarse and plain cotton weave, originally from India, with an attractive natural cream color

CEILING ROSE – decorative molding, fixed centrally in a room, through which a light fitting may be suspended

CHAMFER – narrow, flat surface that has been cut, usually at an angle of 45°, from the corner edge of a post or beam

CHARLESTON – country home, acquired in 1916, of Vanessa Bell and Duncan Grant, and meeting place for other members of the Bloomsbury group. The owners filled the house with exuberant decoration; painting walls, furniture, fabric, and even bathtubs with bold colors and original designs

CHESTERFIELD – large, firmly padded and buttoned sofa with upright arms, often upholstered in leather

CHINOISERIE – seventeenth- and eighteenth-century Western style of decorative art, highly imitative of Oriental designs, that married European forms with exotic, especially Chinese, motifs.

CHINTZ – glazed fabric, closely woven from good quality, medium-weight cotton and traditionally printed with a floral pattern

CLOISONNÉ – type of enamel decoration, in which different-colored enamel is fired in *cloisons* (partitions) separated by flat metal bands, the top edges of which remain visible on the surface of the design.

COIR – coarse fiber from coconut husks, used for ropes and mats

COLONIAL HOUSE – architectural and decorative style of the settlers of New England. The earliest houses only had one downstairs room, often with matchboarding, opening on to a porch, and were furnished with simple, functional pieces made of natural materials

CORNICE – horizontal projection, formed from plaster, wood, metal or even stiffened fabric, used to decorate a wall or conceal curtain fixtures

CRACKLE-GLAZE – decorative glaze effect on ceramics, produced during firing, that leaves a fine network of fissures on the piece of pottery, giving the appearance of age

CREWELWORK – type of needlework in which brilliant-colored wools are embroidered, usually in floral patterns and on light-colored linen backgrounds

D

DADO RAIL – projected molding that runs at about waist-height along a wall, installed both as visual interruption and protection against the knocks of chairs

DAMASK – elegant fabric, generally used for curtains or table linen, in which the lavish pattern is created by the contrasting faces of the same weave

DISTEMPER – paint, formed from mixing pigments with water, glue, size or egg, which used to be used where emulsion paint is used today

DRAWN THREAD WORK – needlework style, in which threads are drawn out from a linen panel and the remaining ones gathered together with embroidery stitches to create a regular, lace-like pattern of holes

DUCK-BOARDING – strips of wood laid over a joint, but with gaps in between them, used on the floor of balconies or verandahs

EF

EMPIRE – French neoclassical style, identified with Emperor Napolean I and reaching its peak in the early-nineteenth century, that sought to include classical ideas with contemporary decorative symbols and that left a lasting influence on furniture, couture and drapery

ESCUTCHEON – ornamental plate or shield that protects the surface surrounding an item such as a keyhole, door handle or light switch

FANLIGHT – semi-circular window, common in Georgian and Regency periods, situated above a door or another window, with glazing bars that resemble the ribs of a fan; nowadays used to describe any shape of window above a door

FESTOON BLIND – eleborate blind comprising a large length of fabric that is gathered up in scallops, suspended between vertical panels, to give a permanently ruched effect

FIESTA WARE – Ceramics produced in the United States in the 1930s with bright, clear, plain colors

GHI

GODIN STOVE – style of wood-burning, workshop stove with an upright, cylindrical design and ornate, pierced-metal decoration

GOUACHE – opaque watercolor paint, the pigments having been fixed with glue, that includes white in its lighter tones

HESSIAN – plainly woven, rough cloth woven from course jute fiber for use in producing bags and upholstery canvas; traditionally used as the backing fabric for hooked rugs

INGLENOOK – recess beside a chimney breast, often with fireside seating

KL

KILIM – smooth, tapestry-woven rug, produced in the Middle East, characterized by its strong patterns and bright colors

LEADED LIGHT – small rectangular or diamond-shaped panes of glass, held in place by a thin, grooved lead strip, that collectively form a window

LOUVER BLIND – hanging blind composed of a series of parallel horizontal slats that can be slanted to overlap and keep out light

M

MARQUETRY – pictorial or patterned veneer, usually fixed to furniture, with an attractive mosaic effect created from shaped pieces of different woods, as well as brass and ivory

MATCHBOARDING – paneling for wall and ceilings comprising long, thin boards, each with a tongue and a groove at opposite edges, that interlock with one another

MULLION – vertical post that separates the panes of glass in a window or the panels in a screen

P

PAMMETS – thick, handmade, semi-vitrified terrocotta tiles that are fired at very high temperatures to give them a tough finish

POINTILLISM – painting technique, inspired by Impressionism, which uses dots of different colors, closely juxtaposed on a white background, to form a series of varying tones when viewed from a distance

POTPOURRI – a mixture of dried leaves, flower petals and other fragrant items stored in an open container to perfume the air

PVA – abbreviation for polyvinyl acetate, a synthetic resin that is the chief ingredient in emulsion paint, giving it durability

R

REGENCY – early-nineteenth-century English neoclassical style, initiated by the Empire style of France, that sought to revive the elegant simplicity of antique models, especially those of Greece. The period witnessed an increase in the use of mahogany and rosewood, a trend towards solidity in furniture and a rebirth of interest in japanned pieces

ROCOCO – early-eighteenth-century style of European decorative art and architecture, originally developed in France, that was characterized by its use of light patterns, pastel colors, delicate proportions and elaborate, abstract motifs, incorporating typically scalloped curves and scrolls

ROLLED-STEEL JOIST (RSJ) – steel beam, structured for strength by its design, which in cross-section reveals the shape of either the letter H or I

ROMAN BLIND – blind that hangs flat when pulled down and that draws up into horizontal pleats

S

SEAGRASS – woven fabric made from seagrasses that is used for table linen and floor mats

SECRETARY – writing cabinet, of French origin, that becomes functional when the hinged, fall-front desk surface, which acts as a door to keep papers safe, is opened down

SETTLE – seat of medieval design, with high arms and back, usually made from wood and often containing a storage space underneath the seat

SHAKERS – popular name, deriving from their excited worship, for church members of the United Society of Believers in Christ's Second Appearing, a sect founded in England in the eighteenth-century but which soon moved to North America. Their furniture is renowned for its grace, simplicity and functional design

SHELLAC – quick-drying, transparent varnish that is used as a barrier coat when painting furniture because it creates a smooth, even surface

SISAL – strong fiber manufactured from assorted *Agave* plants

SPINDLE – long, thin turned piece of wood, with a bulbous swelling about one-third up its length, that collectively can form the back of some styles of Windsor chair

STRETCHER – horizontal crosspiece that connects legs of a table or chair to one another, adding strength

TW

TATTING – technique of cotton or linen lacework, dating back to medieval times, that uses a small hand shuttle to loop the threads

TEMPLATE – thin plate, made from metal, paper or card, that acts as a fixed and accurate guide for cutting out stencils

TIMBER-CLADDING – called clapboard or weatherboard: external wood covering that is applied to a building for both aesthetic and protective purposes

TOILE DE JOUY – type of fabric design, dating back to the eighteenth-century, showing French scenic patterns, depicted in a dark monochrome color on a lighter background

TONGUE-AND-GROOVE JOINT – connection made between two boards by means of a tongue, projecting from an edge of one board, fitting neatly into a groove running along an edge of the other

TRANSOM – horizontal piece of wood that divides window into sections or that separates a door from the window above it

WHATNOT – three or four tiers of square shelving for books or ornaments, supported at the corners by turned spindles; popular in the nineteenth century

A Country House Source List

Sources for country-style furniture, accessories, building supplies, artisans and crafts are virtually endless. Most large department stores (Bloomingdales, Neiman Marcus, Gumps, etc.) carry country furniture (original and reproduction and accessories) and are not included here since stock changes from week to week. Antique shops are not included since quality and stock varies.

This list is intended to provide a working base for anyone in search of particular construction materials, special country decorating furnishings and accessories. Most of the following sources offer mail-order services, and we recommend that you write for catalogs, further information and prices. Every effort has been made to include the most up-to-date and accurate listings.

ART AND CRAFT SUPPLIERS

Chair caning

The Cane-ery
P.O. Box Drawer 17113
Nashville, Tenn. 37217
Chair-caning supplies. Mail-order services.

The Newell Workshop
19 Blaine Avenue
Hinsdale, Ill. 60521
Chair-caning kits and seat-weaving supplies. Mail-order services.

Dried flowers and wreaths

Cherchez
862 Lexington Avenue
New York, N.Y. 10021
Potpourris, sachets; antique linens and other home furnishings.

Delicate Designs
205 Willowgrove South
Tonawanda, N.Y. 14150
Herbal wreaths.

The Newport House
P.O. Box 15415
Richmond, Va. 23227
Floral supplies, wreath forms, dried flowers and herbs.

Needlework

The Hooking Room
1840 House
237 Pine Point Road
Scarborough, Maine 04074
Designs for hooked rugs; kits; supplies.

Jane Snead Samplers
Box 4909
Philadelphia, Pa. 19119
Old-fashioned sampler kits. Mail-order services.

The Stitchery
204 Worcester Street
Wellesley, Mass. 02181
Designs and supplies for knitting, embroidery, quilting, hooked rugs.

Paints

Cohasset Colonials
245X Ship Street
Cohasset, Mass. 02025
Manufacturer of eighteenth- and nineteenth-century reproduction milk-based paints.

Finnaren and Haley, Inc.
2320 Haverford Road
Ardmore, Penn. 19003
Paints in colors of historic Philadelphia and revolutionary era.

The Old Fashioned Milk Paint Company
Box 222
Groton, Mass. 01450
Old-fashioned milk-based paints, wide pine flooring and cabinet boards.

The Olympic Homecare Products Co.
2233 112th Avenue N.E.
Bellevue, Wash. 98004
Traditional paints and stains.

Stencils

Adele Bishop, Inc.
P.O. Box 3349
Kingston, N.C. 28502
Stencil kits for walls and floors; Japan paints, brushes, stencil sheets. Catalog.

The Village Stenciler
25 South Mill Street
Hopkinton, Mass. 07148
Manufacturer of Early American wall and floorcloth stencils. Catalog.

DECORATIVE ACCESSORIES

The American Country Store
969 Lexington Avenue
New York, N.Y. 10021
Antique and contemporary china, flatware, table linens. Mail-order services.

American Folk Art, Ltd.
P.O. Box 5211
Hilton Head, S.C. 29938
Folk art accessories, handcrafted baskets, pot racks, vine wreaths. Catalog.

Ivan Barnett
RD 1
Stevens, Pa. 17578
Original handcrafted weather vanes, Custom work on request. Mail-order services.

Barton's Baskets Etc.
P.O. Box 67
Forkland, Ala. 36740
Assorted Split oak baskets. Mail-order services.

Basketville
Route 1
Putney, Vt. 05346
Handwoven New England ash, oak and native pine baskets. Mail-order services.

The Bayberry
Montauk Highway
Amagansett, N.Y. 11930
Handmade traditional copper weather vanes. Mail-order services.

Bay County Woodcrafts
Route 13
Oak Hall, Va. 23416
Solid pine decorative waterfowl carvings in kit form or finished. Mail-order services.

L.L. Bean, Inc.
Freeport, Maine 04033
Woodburning stoves, decoys, blankets, hammocks, comforters, baskets, cookware, flannel sheets, other rustic items. Mail-order services.

Berea College Student Craft Industries
Berea, Ky. 40403
Handcrafted items, American furniture reproductions, pottery, homespun tablemats, dolls, brooms, baskets. Mail-order services.

Corinne Burke
1 Forest Glen Road
New Paltz, N.Y. 12561
Custom cabinets, Shaker peg racks, dish racks, accessories. Catalog.

Margie Caldwell
Box 1416
Sun Valley, Idaho 83353
Pine-needle baskets. Mail-order services.

The Candle Cellar and Emporium
1914 North Main Street
Fall River, Mass. 02720
Knife and candle boxes that fasten to wall, workmen's tool boxes. Mail-order services.

Coker Creek Crafts
P.O. Box 95
Coker Creek, Tenn. 37314
Traditional and contemporary handmade white oak splint baskets. Mail-order services.

Colonial Williamsburg Foundation
P.O. Box CH
Williamsburg, Va. 23185
Furniture, hardware, dinnerware from Williamsburg Collection. Catalog. Mail-order services.

SOURCE LIST

Cumberland General Store
Route 3
Crossville, Tenn. 38555
Kerosene lamps, sconces, cast-iron cookware, gardening equipment, weather vanes. Mail-order services.

Elizabeth Eakins
1053 Lexington Avenue
New York, N.Y. 10021
Tiles, trays, plates, trivets; custom-made handwoven, braided and hooked rugs.

The Edison Institute
20900 Oakwood Boulevard
Dearborn, Mich 28121
Reproductions from Greenfield Village and Henry Ford Museum including china and other accessories. Mail-order services.

William Hale
P.O. Box 241 DTS
Portland, Maine 04112
Wooden rocking horses. Mail-order services.

Bryant Holsenback
P.O. Box 162
Carrboro, N.C. 27514
Baskets of wild grape, reed, and wisteria. Custom work on request. Mail-order services.

Kay Marshall
2201 Anton Way
Anchorage, Alaska 99503
Handmade denim dolls. Mail-order services.

The Museum of America Folk Art
Museum Shop
62 West 50th Street
New York, N.Y. 10019
Books and objects on traditional American folk art.

Ozark Mountain Collection
7 Downing Street
P.O. Box 507
Hollister, Mo. 65672
Handcrafted pieces: boxes, quilts, furniture.

Joe Panzarella & Jane Byrne Panzarella
High Point Crafts
RD 2. Sky High Road
Tully, N.Y. 13159
Woven fireplace brooms, feather dusters, bellows.

Barbara and Daniel Strawser
125 Main Street and Stouchsburg
Womelsdorf, Pa. 19567
Folk paintings, wood carvings. Mail-order services.

Winterthur Museum Reproductions
Winterthur
Delaware 19735
Hardware, pottery, china, furniture, accessories. Mail-order services.

The Yankee Peddler
Burkart Brothers Inc.
Verplanck, N.Y. 10596
Colonial reproduction tinware accessories, lanterns, saltboxes, candlesticks. Mail-order services. Catalog.

BUILDING MATERIALS AND SUPPLIES

Ceiling fans

Casablanca Fan Company
450 North Baldwin Park Boulevard
City of Industry, Calif. 91746
Ceiling fans, kitchen fixtures. Catalog available.

Flooring, molding, paneling, and wood details

Broad-Axe Beam
RD 2 Box 417
West Brattleboro, Vt. 05301
Hand-hewn white pine beams, structural and decorative.

Cape Cod Cupola Company
78 State Road, Route 6
North Dartmouth, Mass. 02747
Cupolas.

Carlisle Restoration Lumber
Route 123
Stoddard, N.H. 03464
Wide pine and oak flooring, paneling. Mail-order services.

Driwood Moulding Company
P.O. Box 1729
Florence, S.C. 29503
Period millwork, embossed and plain molding. Catalog.

Forms & Surfaces
Box 5215
Santa Barbara, Calif. 93108
Country wood cabinet pulls and carved wood cabinetry panels.

Guyon Industries, Inc.
65 Oak Street
Lititz, Pa. 17543
Rustic wood products: Barn siding, pine clapboard siding, rustic fencing, hewn beams and timbers, wide plank pine flooring primitive furniture; settler's cabins.

The House Carpenters
Box 217
Shutesbury, Mass. 01072
Traditional red-oak and white-pine timber frame, eighteenth-century flooring, molding, paneling, doors and doorways, windows.

Maurer & Shepherd, Joyners
122 Naubuc Avenue
Glastonbury, Conn. 06033
Colonial-style small pane windows, sashes and frames, wide pine flooring. Custom work on request.

E.A. Nord Company
P.O. Box 1187
Everett, Wash. 98206
Hemlock and fir louvered, bifold, and six-panel doors.

W.F. Norman
P.O. Box 323
Nevada, Mo. 64772
Authentic tin ceilings, roof shingels, siding. Catalog.

The Old Fashioned Milk Paint Company
Box 222
Groton, Mass. 01450
Wide pine flooring and cabinet boards, old-fashioned milk paints.

Old World Moulding & Finishing Company, Inc.
115 Allen Boulevard
Farmingdale, N.Y. 11735
Custom architectural paneling, woodwork, mantels, wall units.

Period Pine, Inc.
#6 North Rhodes Center N.W.
Atlanta, Ga. 30309
Old virgin long-leaf yellow pine, flooring, paneling, millwork.

Restorations Unlimited
P.O. Box 186
24 West Main
Elizabethville, Pa. 17023
Restoration consultation and period millwork.

Wood Moulding & Millwork Producers Association
P.O. Box 25278
Portland, Oreg. 997225
Trade association representing unfinished-wood molding manufacturers; booklets on use, installations, and how-to of wood products available.

FURNITURE

Amish Country Collection
R.D. 5
Sunset Valley Road
New Castle, Pa. 16105
Willow and slat furniture.

Bedlam Brass Beds
19-21 Fairlawn Avenue
Fair Lawn, N.J. 07410
Brass beds. Parts for restoration of antique brass beds. Custom designs on request.

Bittersweet
P.O. Box 5
Riverton, Vt. 05668
Handcrafted American primitive furniture, cupboards, grandfather clocks, tables. Custom work on request.

Christopher Design
3701 Turtle Creek Boulevard
Dallas, Tex. 75219
Twig furniture.

Colonial Williamsburg Foundation
P.O. Box C11
Williamsburg, Va. 23185
Furniture, fabrics, wallcoverings, lighting, etc. Mail-order services.

Craig Nutt Fine Wood Works
2014 5th Street
Northport, Ala. 35476
Traditional American furniture. Custom work on request.

186

SOURCE LIST

Guild of Shaker Crafts
401 W. Savidge
Spring Lake, Mich. 49456
Authentic Shaker replicas: backslat benches, trestle tables, oval boxes, chests, chairs, beds, brooms, Shaker pegs and knobs.

Habersham Plantation
P.O. Box 1209
Toccoa, Ga. 30577
Manufacturer of American primitive furniture: hutch tables, cupboards, pie safes, shelving, ladderback chairs, sleigh beds, tavern beds, canopy beds, chests.

Historic Charleston Reproductions
105 Broad Street
Charleston, S.C. 29401
Furniture, fabrics, china, accessories. Mail-order services.

The Rocker Shop
of Marietta Georgia
1421 White Circle, N.W.
P.O. Box 12
Marietta, Ga. 30061
Brumby rocker with matching footstool; child's rocker, dining chairs, porch swings.

Shaker Workshops, Inc.
Box 1028
Concord, Mass. 01742
Shaker furniture kits. Mail-order services.

HARDWARE

Cassidy Brothers Forge
Route 1
Rowley, Mass. 01969
Wrought-iron fireplace tools and accessories, hardware, architectural ironwork. Mail-order services.

John Graney
Bear Creek Forge
Route 2 Box 135
Spring Green, Wis. 53588
Decorative and functional ironwork; and irons, Colonial cooking hardware, kitchen racks, triangle dinner gongs. Custom work on request. Mail-order services.

Steve Hayne Hand Forged Hardware
17 Harmon Place
Smithtown, N.Y. 11787
Fireplace tools and accessories; forged steel, brass, copper; military accouterments; builder's hardware; hand-cast brass and bronze; household hardware: repairs, restorations. Mail-order services.

Old Guildford Forge
1840 Boston Post Road
Guildford, Conn. 06437
Hand-forged wrought-iron products; fireplace equipment. Mail-order services.

Wallin Forge
Route 1 Box 65
Sparta, Ky. 41086
Hand-forged ironware: utensil and pot racks, fireplace accessories, hardware. Custom work on request. Mail-order services.

KITCHEN AND BATHROOM FIXTURES

Bathroom fixtures

Baldwin/Tubs, Inc.
At the head of Morgan Bay
Surry, Maine 04684
Handcrafted wooden tubs.

Fife's Woodworking and Manufacturing
Route 107
Northwood, N.H. 03261
Handcrafted solid wood bathroom accessories. Custom woodworking on request. Mail-order services.

The Tile Shop
1577 Solano Avenue
Berkeley, Calif. 94704
Stoneware sinks. Custom work on request. Mail-order services.

Kitchen appliances

Comforter Stove Works
Box 175
Lochmere, N.H. 03252
Woodburning stoves for heating.

Quaker Stove Co., Inc.
200 West Fifth Street
Lansdale, Pa. 19446
Woodburning stoves for heating.

Stanley Iron Works
64 Taylor Street
Nashua, N.H. 03060
Antique cookstoves.

Washington Stove Works
P.O. Box 687
Everett, Wash. 98201
Potbelly stoves for heating and cooking.

LIGHTING

Antiquity Handcrafted Artifacts Inc.
255 North Aaron Street
Eaton, Ohio 45320
Early American lighting fixtures: sconces, lanterns, candlesticks, chandeliers, tinware. Mail-order services.

Electric Candle Mfg. Co.
60 Chelmsford Street
Chelmsford, Mass. 01824
Beeswax candle covers, electric candles and bulbs. Mail-order services.

Hurley Patentee Manor
RD7 Box 98A
Kingston, N.Y. 12401
Handcrafted reproductions of 18th- and 19th century lighting fixtures. Mail-order services.

Jori Hand Cast Pewter
Bucks County Pewterers, Inc.
P.O. Box 157
Jamison, Pa. 18929
Hand-cast traditional pewter candlesticks and sconces. Mail-order services.

Charles Lapen
Route 9 P.O. Box 529
West Brookfield, Mass. 01585
Hand-forged colonial reproduction chandeliers and candle stands. Custom work on request. Mail-order services.

Mad River Pottery
RFD/Box 28
Bristol, Vt. 05443
Stoneware chandeliers. Mail-order services.

Patti Brothers
Village Green
Route 27
Sudbury, Mass. 01776
Early American lighting fixtures: chandeliers, sconces, lamps, candlesticks. Custom work on request. Mail-order services.

Period Lighting Fixtures
1 Main Street
Chester, Conn. 06412
Handmade reproductions of early American lanterns, chandeliers, sconces. Mail-order services.

WALLCOVERINGS, FABRICS AND FLOOR TREATMENTS

Adams and Swett
380 Dorchester Avenue
Boston, Mass. 02127
Traditional handbraided wool rugs. Mail-order services.

Carol Brown
Boxway
Putney, Vt. 05346
Irish tweeds and natural fiber fabrics for upholsters and curtains. Mail-order services.

Craftswomen
Box 715
Doylestown, Pa. 18901
Custom-made canvas floorcloths based on early patterns. Mail-order services.

Floorcloths Incorporated
P.O. Box 812
Severna Park, Md. 21146
Custom-made canvas floorcloths in documented patterns. Mail-order services.

Alice Pickett, Handweaver
194 Chestnut Street
Rehoboth, Mass 02769
Custom-designed handwoven rugs. Mail-order services.

Puckihuddle Products, Ltd.
Box AW 5
Aliverea, N.Y. 12462
Amish hand-loomed rugs. Mail-order services.

Tim and Maureen Rastetter
Rastetter Woolen Mill
Star Route
Millsburg, Ohio 44654
Handmade rag rugs and rag carpeting. Mail-order services.

INDEX

Acknowledgments

DORLING KINDERSLEY would like to thank the following suppliers for loan or hire of materials photographed in the book (full addresses are given at the first mention of each supplier):

Fabrics (29 and 102–3)

The Antique Textile Company, 100 Portland Road, London W11 4LQ: Antique paisley, cotton candlewick bedcover, indigo check eiderdown cover, crewelwork embroidery bedcover.

Ghiordes Knot, 11 Freegrove Road, London N7: Turkish rug.

Putnams Collections Ltd, Mathews Yard, 29 Shorts Gardens, London WC2H 9AP: blue and white cotton.

Flooring (46–7)

DLW (Britain) Ltd, Block 38C, Milton Park Estate, Abingdon, Oxon OX14 4RT: Linoleum.

Fired Earth, 37–41 Battersea High Street, London SW11 3JF: Octagonal terracota tile, terracotta lozenge, glazed pavers, octagonal slate tile.

The London Architectural Salvage and Supply Co. Ltd, St Michael's and All Angels, Mark Street, London EC2A 4ER: Elm and oak boards, oak parquet, square and hexagonal terracotta quarry tiles, encaustic tile, marble tiles and slabs, York stone slab.

Paris Ceramics, 243 Battersea Park Road, London SW11 3BL: Rectangular terracotta tile, blue English limestone tile, French limestone flag, animal ceramic tile.

Plumbing fixtures (56–7)

Czech and Speake, 244–254 Cambridge Heath Road, London E2 9DA: Sink mixer, sponge rack, lavatory paper roll holder, bath tap, bath mixer with handshower, single robe hook.

Fired Earth: Mexican handmade tiles, Italian border tiles.

Habitat, The Heals Building, 196 Tottenham Court Road, London W1P 9LD: Porcelain toothbrush holder.

T A Harris, Hargreen House, 134 New Kent Road, London SE1 6TY: Belfast sink.

C P Hart, Newnham Terrace, Hercules Road, London SE1: Cistern, lavatory seat cover, hand-basin and taps, towel rail, cistern levers, porcelain pull handle.

The London Architectural Salvage and Supply Co. Ltd: Lavatory paper dispenser.

David Mellor, 26 James Street, London WC2E 8PA: Plate rack.

Kerry von Zschock, Maiolica Tiles, Ruskin Mill, Old Bristol Road, Nailsworth, Gloucestershire: Border tiles, fish tiles.

Lighting (64–5)

John Allsop Antiques, 26 Pimlico Road, London SW1: Painted tin candlestick lamp bases.

Bennison, 91 Pimlico Road, London SW1: Mahogany candlestick lamp base.

Habitat: Ceramic wall light.

Anna Lambert Decorated Earthenware, 10 High Oaks Road, Welwyn Garden City, Hertfordshire: Decorated earthenware candlestick.

Lloyd Adamson, Pastiche Lamps, 13 Henning Street, London SW11 3DR: Pastiche lamp.

The London Architectural Salvage and Supply Co. Ltd: Large paraffin lamp.

Vaughan, 156–160 Wandsworth Bridge Road, London SW6 2UH: Georgian woodlen candlestick lamp base, Kashmiri candlestick, brass candlestick lamp base.

Woods Electrical Accessories, Goodleigh House, Blackborough, Cullompton, Devon EX15 2JA: Light switches.

Woolpit Interiors, The Street, Woolpit, Bury St Edmunds, Suffolk IP30 9SA: Painted wooden lamp base.

Christopher Wray's Lighting Emporium, 600 King's Road, London SW6 2DX: Hanging shade, swing-arm wall bracket, knuckle unit, ceiling hooks, rise and fall pendant, trough lamp.

Door and window fittings (68–9)

J D Beardmore and Co. Ltd, 3 and 4 Percy Street, London W1P 0EJ: Iron casement stay, black iron hinges, brass escutcheon.

The London Architectural Salvage and Supply Co. Ltd: Sliding casement stay, blind pull, brass and cord knob, window shutter, brass door handle, brass and porcelain door knob, wood and brass door knobs, painted glass door panel, leaded light, brass loop handle, enamel door number, ceramic escutcheon, French window sliding bolt, black finger plate.

Sainsbury's Homebase Ltd, Warwick Road, London W14: Curtain poles and rings.

Vaughan: Brass tie back.

ACKNOWLEDGMENTS

Yannedis and Co. Ltd, 25–27 Theobalds Road, London WC1: Brass window latch, brass casement and quadrant stays, cleat-hook, brass door hinge, black iron door handle, brass door knob, cabin hook.

Decorating tools (76–7 and 160)

Ardenbrite Products Ltd, 57 Farringdon Road, London EC1M 3JH: Eggshell paint, paint tray, spray paints.

Brodie and Middleton Ltd, 68 Drury Lane, London WC2B 5SP: Modeling knife, wallpaper brush, oiled manila paper, paint bucket.

Buck and Ryan Ltd, 101 Tottenham Court Road, London W1: Household brushes, sandpaper, sanding blocks, white spirit, yacht varnish, plumb line, workbench.

L Cornelissen and Son Ltd, 105 Great Russell Street, London WC1B 3RY: Varnishing brush, mahl stick, large stencil brush, combs.

Robert Dyas Ltd, 97 St Martin's Lane, London WC2: Emulsion paints.

London Graphic Centre, 107–115 Long Acre, London WC2E 9NT: Acetate pad, acetate roll, cutting mat, craft knives, art paper, masking tape, cutting ruler, scissors, felt-tipped pens, pencil.

George Rowney and Co. Ltd, 12 Percy Street, London W1A: Powder paints, small paint brushes, softening brush, dragging brush, small stencil brushes, acrylic oil paints.

Furniture fittings (120–1)

J D Beardmore and Co. Ltd: drop ring cabinet handle, black iron cabinet handle, cabinet escutcheon, snake hinges, "H" hinges.

The London Architectural Salvage and Supply Co. Ltd: Glass cabinet knob, toggle fastener.

Sainsbury's Homebase Ltd: White ceramic knobs.

Yannedis and Co. Ltd: Brass cabinet handle, brass cabinet knob.

DORLING KINDERSLEY would like to thank the following people for allowing their homes to be photographed: Miles and Lillian Cahn, Mr and Mrs John Fell-Clarke, Rena Forman, Don and Leslie Hastings, Malcolm Hillier, Sheran and Stephen James, Katherine Martucci, Thane and Catherine Meldrum, Paul Nix, Sid and Joan Osofsky, Mr and Mrs Michael Pepper, Annie Sloan, Andrew and Joanna Young.

DORLING KINDERSLEY would like to thank the following people for their help in producing this book:

Duncan Bayliss (step-by-step sequences), **Hilary Bird** (indexer) and **Tracey Orme** (photographic assistant).

Illustrations by **Eric Thomas**.
Additional illustrations by **Marion Appleton**: pages 164 (cornices), 167–9 (bath), 169 (valance), 170–1 (table), 177 (chest), 178 (chair); and **Mustafa Sami**: pages 173–5 (workstand), 175–6 (dresser).

Special thanks also to:
Penny Black, Konrad Child, Rosie Ford, Malcolm Hillier, Mark James, Laura Overton, Richmond Antique Traders, John Smallwood, Roger Smoothy.

AUTHOR'S ACKNOWLEDGMENTS
Special thanks to Roger and Leo and Spigs, who put up with being dragged and distressed.
And to Spike, David, Nick and Josie, who did all the rest.

Thanks also to Deirdre McSharry, Jocasta and Margaret Caselton for providing inspiration.